Yours very truly
E. Howard.

GARDEN CITIES

OF

TO-MORROW

GARDEN CITIES

OF

TO-MORROW

(BEING THE SECOND EDITION OF "TO-MORROW: A PEACEFUL PATH TO REAL REFORM")

BY

EBENEZER HOWARD

" New occasions teach new duties;
Time makes ancient good uncouth;
They must upward still, and onward,
Who would keep abreast of truth.
Lo, before us, gleam her camp-fires !
We ourselves must pilgrims be,
Launch our Mayflower, and steer boldly
Through the desperate winter sea,
Nor attempt the Future's portal
With the past's blood-rusted key,"

ISBN: 978-93-5128-863-3(HB)

First Published in 1902
Indian Reprint in 2017

Published by

Kalpaz Publications
C-30, Satyawati Nagar,
Delhi – 110052
E-mail: kalpaz@hotmail.com
Website: kalpazpublications.com
Ph.: +91-9212142040

Cataloging in Publication Data—DK
Courtesy: D.K. Agencies (P) Ltd. <docinfo@dkagencies.com>

Howard, Ebenezer, *Sir,* 1850-1928**, author.**
[Tomorrow]
Garden cities of to-morrow : being the second edition of "To-morrow: a peaceful path to real reform" / by Ebenezer Howard.
pages cm
Reprint. Originally published: London : Swan Sonnenschein & Co., Ltd., 1902.
ISBN 9789351288633

1. Garden cities. I. Title.

HT161.H6 2017 DDC 307.1216 23

CONTENTS

LIST OF ILLUSTRATIONS

GARDEN CITIES OF TO-MORROW.

INTRODUCTION.

"New forces, new cravings, new aims, which had been silently gathering beneath the crust of re-action, burst suddenly into view."—Green's "Short History of the English People," Chap. x.

"Change is consummated in many cases after much argument and agitation, and men do not observe that almost everything has been silently effected by causes to which few people paid any heed. In one generation an institution is unassailable, in the next bold men may assail it, and in the third bold men defend it. At one time the most conclusive arguments are advanced against it in vain, if indeed they are allowed utterance at all. At another time the most childish sophistry is enough to secure its condemnation. In the first place, the institution, though probably indefensible by pure reason, was congruous with the conscious habits and modes of thought of the community. In the second, these had changed from influences which the acutest analysis would probably fail to explain, and a breath sufficed to topple over the sapped structure."—*The Times*, 27th November, 1891.

In these days of strong party feeling and of keenly-contested social and religious issues, it might perhaps be thought difficult to find a single question having a vital bearing upon national life and well-being on which all persons, no matter of what political party, or of what shade of sociological opinion, would be found to be fully and entirely agreed. Discuss the temperance cause, and you will hear from Mr. John Morley that it is "the greatest moral movement since the movement for the abolition of slavery"; but Lord Bruce will remind you that "every year the trade contributes £40,000,000 to the revenue of the country, so that practically it maintains the Army and Navy, besides which it affords employment to many thousands of persons"—that "even the teetotalers owe much to the licensed victuallers, for if it were not for them the refreshment bars at the Crystal Palace would have been closed long ago." Discuss the opium traffic, and, on the one hand, you will hear that opium is rapidly destroying the *morale* of the people of China, and, on the other, that this is quite a delusion, and that the Chinese are capable, thanks to opium, of doing work which to a European is quite impossible, and that on food at which the least squeamish of English people would turn up their noses in disgust.

Religious and political questions too often divide us into hostile camps; and so, in the very realms where calm, dispassionate thought and pure emotions are the essentials of all advance towards right beliefs and sound principles of action, the din of battle and the struggles of contending hosts are more forcibly suggested to the onlooker than the really sincere love of truth and love of country which, one may yet be sure, animate nearly all breasts.

There is, however, a question in regard to which one can scarcely find any difference of opinion. It is well-nigh universally agreed by men of all parties, not only in England, but all over Europe and America and our colonies, that it is deeply to be deplored that the people should continue to stream into the already over-crowded cities, and should thus further deplete the country districts.

Lord Rosebery, speaking some years ago as Chairman of the London County Council, dwelt with very special emphasis on this point:—

"There is no thought of pride associated in my mind with the idea of London. I am always haunted by the awfulness of London: by the great appalling fact of these millions cast down, as it would appear by hazard, on the banks of this noble stream, working each in their own groove and their own cell, without regard or knowledge of each other, without heeding each other, without having the slightest idea how the other lives—the heedless casualty of unnumbered thousands of men. Sixty years ago a great Englishman, Cobbett, called it a wen. If it was a wen then, what is it now? A tumour, an elephantiasis sucking into its gorged system half the life and the blood and the bone of the rural districts."—March, 1891.

Sir John Gorst points out the evil, and suggests the remedy:

"If they wanted a permanent remedy of the evil they must remove the cause; they must back the tide, and stop the migration of the people into the towns, and get the people back to the land. The interest and the safety of the towns themselves were involved in the solution of the problem."—*Daily Chronicle*, 6th November, 1891.

Dean Farrar says:

"We are becoming a land of great cities. Villages are stationary or receding; cities are enormously increasing. And if it be true that great cities tend more and more to become the graves of the physique of our race, can we wonder at it when we see the houses so foul, so squalid, so ill-drained, so vitiated by neglect and dirt?"

Dr. Rhodes, at the Demographic Congress, called attention to

"the migration which was going on from the English agricultural districts. In Lancashire and other manufacturing districts 35 per cent. of the population were over 60 years of age, but in agricultural districts they would have over 60 per cent. Many of the cottages were so abominable that they could not call them houses, and the people so deteriorated in physique that they were not able to do the amount of work which able-bodied persons should do. Unless something was done to make the lot of the agricultural labourer better, the exodus would go on, with what results in the future he dared not say."—*Times*, 15th August, 1891.

The Press, Liberal, Radical, and Conservative, views this grave symptom of the time with the same alarm. The *St. James's Gazette*, on June 6, 1892, remarks:

"How best to provide the proper antidote against the greatest danger of modern existence is a question of no mean significance."

The Star, 9th October, 1891, says:

"How to stem the drift from the country is one of the main problems of the day. The labourer may perhaps be restored to the land, but how will the country industries be restored to rural England?"

The Daily News, a few years ago, published a series of articles, "Life in our Villages," dealing with the same problem.

Trade Unionist leaders utter the same note of warning. Mr. Ben Tillet says:

"Hands are hungry for toil, and lands are starving for labour."

Mr. Tom Mann observes:

"The congestion of labour in the metropolis is caused mainly by the influx from the country districts of those who were needed there to cultivate the land."

All, then, are agreed on the pressing nature of this problem, all are bent on its solution, and though it would doubtless be quite Utopian to expect a similar agreement as to the value of any remedy that may be proposed, it is at least of immense importance that, on a subject thus universally regarded as of supreme importance, we have such a consensus of opinion at the outset. This will be the more remarkable and the more hopeful sign when it is shown, as I believe will be conclusively shown in this work, that the answer to this, one of the most pressing questions of the day, makes of comparatively easy solution many other problems which have hitherto taxed the ingenuity of the greatest thinkers and reformers of our time. Yes, the key to the problem how to restore the people to the land—that beautiful land of ours, with its canopy of sky, the air that blows upon it, the sun that warms it, the rain and dew that moisten it—the very embodiment of Divine love for man—is indeed a *Master-Key,* for it is the key to a portal through which, even when scarce ajar, will be seen to pour a flood of light on the problems of intemperance, of excessive toil, of restless anxiety, of grinding poverty—the true limits of Governmental interference, ay, and even the relations of man to the Supreme Power.

It may perhaps be thought that the first step to be taken towards the solution of this question—how to restore the people to the land—would involve a careful consideration of the very numerous causes which have hitherto led to their aggregation in large cities. Were this the case, a very prolonged enquiry would be necessary at the outset. Fortunately, alike for writer and for reader, such an analysis is not, however, here requisite, and for a very simple reason, which may be stated thus: —Whatever may have been the causes which have operated in the past, and are operating now, to draw the people into the cities, those causes may all be summed up as "attractions"; and it is obvious, therefore, that no remedy can possibly be effective which will not present to the people, or at least to considerable portions of them, greater "attractions" than our cities now possess, so that the force of the old "attractions" shall be overcome by the force of new "attractions" which are to be created. Each city may be regarded as a magnet, each person as a needle; and, so viewed, it is at once seen that nothing short of the discovery of a method for constructing magnets of yet greater power than our cities possess can be effective for re-distributing the population in a spontaneous and healthy manner.

So presented, the problem may appear at first sight to be difficult, if not impossible, of solution. "What," some may be disposed to ask, "can possibly be done to make the country more attractive to a work-a-day people than the town—to make wages, or at least the standard of physical comfort, higher in the country than in the town; to secure in the country equal possibilities of social intercourse, and to make the prospects of advancement for the average man or woman equal, not to say superior, to those enjoyed in our large cities?" The issue one constantly finds presented in a form very similar to that. The subject is treated continually in the public press, and in all forms of discussion, as though men, or at least working-men, had not now, and never could have, any choice or alternative, but either, on the one hand, to stifle their love for human society—at least in wider relations than can be found in a straggling village—or, on the other hand, to forego almost entirely all the keen and pure delights of the country. The question is universally considered as though it were now, and for ever must remain, quite impossible for working people to live in the country and yet be engaged in pursuits other than agricultural; as though crowded, unhealthy cities were the last word of economic science; and as if our present form of industry, in which sharp lines divide agricultural from industrial pursuits, were necessarily an enduring one. This fallacy is the very common one of ignoring altogether the possibility of alternatives other than those presented to the mind. There are in reality not only, as is so constantly assumed, two alternatives—town life and country life—but a third alternative, in which all the advantages of the most energetic and active town life, with all the beauty and delight of the country, may be secured in perfect combination; and the certainty of being able to live this life will be the magnet which will produce the effect for which we are all striving—the spontaneous movement of the people from our crowded cities to the bosom of our kindly mother earth, at once the source of life, of happiness, of wealth, and of power. The town and the country may, therefore, be regarded as two magnets, each striving to draw the people to itself—a rivalry which a new form of life, partaking of the nature of both, comes to take part in. This may be illustrated by a diagram of "The Three Magnets," in which the chief advantages of the Town and of the Country are set forth with their corresponding drawbacks, while the advantages of the Town-Country are seen to be free from the disadvantages of either.

The Town magnet, it will be seen, offers, as compared with the Country magnet, the advantages of high wages, opportunities for employment, tempting prospects of advancement, but these are largely counterbalanced by high rents and prices. Its social opportunities and its places of amusement are very alluring, but excessive hours of toil, distance from work, and the "isolation of crowds" tend greatly to reduce the value of these good things. The well-lit streets are a great attraction, especially in winter, but the sunlight is being more and more shut out, while the air is so vitiated that the fine public buildings, like the sparrows, rapidly become covered with soot, and the very statues are in despair. Palatial edifices and fearful slums are the strange, complementary features of modern cities.

The Country magnet declares herself to be the source of all beauty and wealth; but the Town magnet mockingly reminds her that she is very dull for lack of society, and very sparing of her gifts for lack of capital. There are in the country beautiful vistas, lordly parks, violet-scented woods, fresh air, sounds of rippling water; but too often one sees those threatening words, "Trespassers will be prosecuted." Rents, if estimated by the acre, are certainly low, but such low rents are the natural fruit of low wages rather than a cause of substantial comfort; while long hours and lack of amusements forbid the bright sunshine and the pure air to gladden the hearts

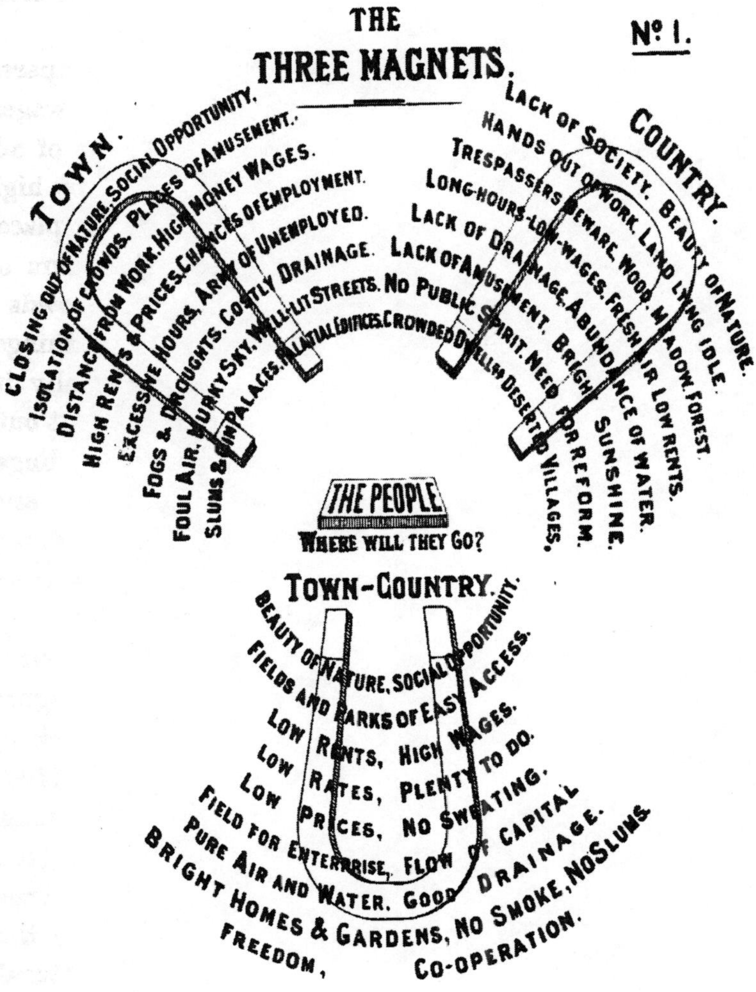
THE
THREE MAGNETS.
No. 1.
TOWN.
CLOSING OUT OF NATURE. SOCIAL OPPORTUNITY.
ISOLATION OF CROWDS. PLACES OF AMUSEMENT.
DISTANCE FROM WORK. HIGH MONEY WAGES.
HIGH RENTS & PRICES. CHANCES OF EMPLOYMENT.
EXCESSIVE HOURS. ARMY OF UNEMPLOYED.
FOGS & DROUGHTS. COSTLY DRAINAGE.
FOUL AIR. MURKY SKY. WELL-LIT STREETS.
SLUMS & GIN PALACES. PALATIAL EDIFICES.
COUNTRY.
LACK OF SOCIETY. BEAUTY OF NATURE.
HANDS OUT OF WORK. LAND LYING IDLE.
TRESPASSERS BEWARE. WOOD, MEADOW, FOREST.
LONG HOURS-LOW WAGES. FRESH AIR. LOW RENTS.
LACK OF DRAINAGE. ABUNDANCE OF WATER.
LACK OF AMUSEMENT. BRIGHT SUNSHINE.
NO PUBLIC SPIRIT. NEED FOR REFORM.
CROWDED DWELLINGS. DESERTED VILLAGES.
THE PEOPLE
WHERE WILL THEY GO?
TOWN-COUNTRY.
BEAUTY OF NATURE. SOCIAL OPPORTUNITY.
FIELDS AND PARKS OF EASY ACCESS.
LOW RENTS, HIGH WAGES.
LOW RATES, PLENTY TO DO.
LOW PRICES, NO SWEATING.
FIELD FOR ENTERPRISE, FLOW OF CAPITAL.
PURE AIR AND WATER. GOOD DRAINAGE.
BRIGHT HOMES & GARDENS, NO SMOKE, NO SLUMS.
FREEDOM, CO-OPERATION.

of the people. The one industry, agriculture, suffers frequently from excessive rainfalls; but this wondrous harvest of the clouds is seldom properly ingathered, so that, in times of drought, there is frequently, even for drinking purposes, a most insufficient supply.[1] Even the natural healthfulness of the country is largely lost for lack of proper drainage and other sanitary conditions, while, in parts almost deserted by the people, the few who remain are yet frequently huddled together as if in rivalry with the slums of our cities.

But neither the Town magnet nor the Country magnet represents the full plan and purpose of nature. Human society and the beauty of nature are meant to be enjoyed together. The two magnets must be made one. As man and woman by their varied gifts and faculties supplement each other, so should town and country. The town is the symbol of society—of mutual help and friendly co-operation, of fatherhood, motherhood, brotherhood, sisterhood, of wide relations between man and man—of broad, expanding sympathies—of science, art, culture, religion. And the country! The country is the symbol of God's

[1] Dr. Barwise, Medical Officer of Health for the County Council of Derbyshire, giving evidence before a Select Committee of the House of Commons, on 25th April, 1894, on the Chesterfield Gas and Water Bill, said, in answer to Question 1873: "At Brimington Common School I saw some basins full of soapsuds, and it was all the water that the whole of the children had to wash in. They had to wash one after another in the same water. Of course, a child with ringworm or something of that kind might spread it through the whole of the children. . . . The schoolmistress told me that the children came in from the playground hot, and she had seen them actually drink this dirty water. In fact, when they were thirsty there was no other water for them to have."

love and care for man. All that we are and all that we have comes from it. Our bodies are formed of it; to it they return. We are fed by it, clothed by it, and by it are we warmed and sheltered. On its bosom we rest. Its beauty is the inspiration of art, of music, of poetry. Its forces propel all the wheels of industry. It is the source of all health, all wealth, all knowledge. But its fulness of joy and wisdom has not revealed itself to man. Nor can it ever, so long as this unholy, unnatural separation of society and nature endures. Town and country *must be married*, and out of this joyous union will spring a new hope, a new life, a new civilisation. It is the purpose of this work to show how a first step can be taken in this direction by the construction of a Town-country magnet; and I hope to convince the reader that this is practicable, here and now, and that on principles which are the very soundest, whether viewed from the ethical or the economic standpoint.

I will undertake, then, to show how in "Town-country" equal, nay better, opportunities of social intercourse may be enjoyed than are enjoyed in any crowded city, while yet the beauties of nature may encompass and enfold each dweller therein; how higher wages are compatible with reduced rents and rates; how abundant opportunities for employment and bright prospects of advancement may be secured for all; how capital may be attracted and wealth created; how the most admirable sanitary conditions may be ensured; how beautiful homes and gardens may be seen on every hand; how the bounds of freedom may be widened, and yet all the best results of concert and co-operation gathered in by a happy people.

The construction of such a magnet, could it be effected, followed, as it would be, by the construction of many more, would certainly afford a solution of the burning question set before us by Sir John Gorst, "how to back the tide of migration of the people into the towns, and to get them back upon the land."

A fuller description of such a magnet and its mode of construction will form the theme of subsequent chapters.

CHAPTER I.

THE TOWN-COUNTRY MAGNET.

"I will not cease from mental strife,
 Nor shall my sword sleep in my hand,
Till we have built Jerusalem
 In England's green and pleasant land."

—*Blake*.

"Thorough sanitary and remedial action in the houses that we have; and then the building of more, strongly, beautifully, and in groups of limited extent, kept in proportion to their streams and walled round, so that there may be no festering and wretched suburb anywhere, but clean and busy street within and the open country without, with a belt of beautiful garden and orchard round the walls, so that from any part of the city perfectly fresh air and grass and sight of far horizon might be reachable in a few minutes' walk. This the final aim."—John Ruskin, "Sesame and Lilies."

The reader is asked to imagine an estate embracing an area of 6,000 acres, which is at present purely agricultural, and has been obtained by purchase in the open market at a cost of £40[1] an acre, or £240,000. The purchase money is supposed to have been raised on mortgage debentures, bearing interest at an average rate not ex-

[1] This was the average price paid for agricultural land in 1898: and, though this estimate may prove far more than sufficient, it is hardly likely to be much exceeded.

ceeding £4 per cent.[1] The estate is legally vested in the names of four gentlemen of responsible position and of undoubted probity and honour, who hold it in trust, first, as a security for the debenture-holders, and, secondly, in trust for the people of Garden City, the Town-country magnet, which it is intended to build thereon. One essential feature of the plan is that all ground rents, which are to be based upon the annual value of the land, shall be paid to the trustees, who, after providing for interest and sinking fund, will hand the balance to the Central Council of the new municipality,[2] to be employed by such Council in the creation and maintenance of all necessary public works—roads, schools, parks, etc.

The objects of this land purchase may be stated in various ways, but it is sufficient here to say that some of the chief objects are these: To find for our industrial population work at wages of *higher purchasing power*, and to secure healthier surroundings and more regular employment. To enterprising manufacturers, co-operative societies, architects, engineers, builders, and mechanicians of all kinds, as well as to many engaged in various professions, it is intended to offer a means of securing new and better employment for their capital and talents, while to the agriculturists at present on the estate, as well as to those who may migrate

[1] The financial arrangements described in this book are likely to be departed from in form, but not in essential principle. And until a definite scheme has been agreed upon, I think it better to repeat them precisely as they appeared in "To-Morrow," the original title of this book—the book which led to the formation of the Garden City Association. See Appendix.

[2] This word, "municipality," is not used in a technical sense.

thither, it is designed to open a new market for their produce close to their doors. Its object is, in short, to raise the standard of health and comfort of all true workers of whatever grade—the means by which these objects are to be achieved being a healthy, natural, and economic combination of town and country life, and this on land owned by the municipality.

Garden City, which is to be built near the centre of the 6,000 acres, covers an area of 1,000 acres, or a sixth part of the 6,000 acres, and might be of circular form, 1,240 yards (or nearly three-quarters of a mile) from centre to circumference. (Diagram 2 is a ground-plan of the whole municipal area, showing the town in the centre; and Diagram 3, which represents one section or ward of the town, will be useful in following the description of the town itself—**a description which is, however, merely suggestive, and will probably be much departed from.**)

Six magnificent boulevards—each 120 feet wide—traverse the city from centre to circumference, dividing it into six equal parts or wards. In the centre is a circular space containing about five and a half acres, laid out as a beautiful and well-watered garden; and, surrounding this garden, each standing in its own ample grounds, are the larger public buildings—town hall, principal concert and lecture hall, theatre, library, museum, picture-gallery, and hospital.

The rest of the large space encircled by the "Crystal Palace" is a public park, containing 145 acres, which includes ample recreation grounds within very easy access of all the people.

Running all round the Central Park (except where it

— Nº 2. —

GARDEN-CITY

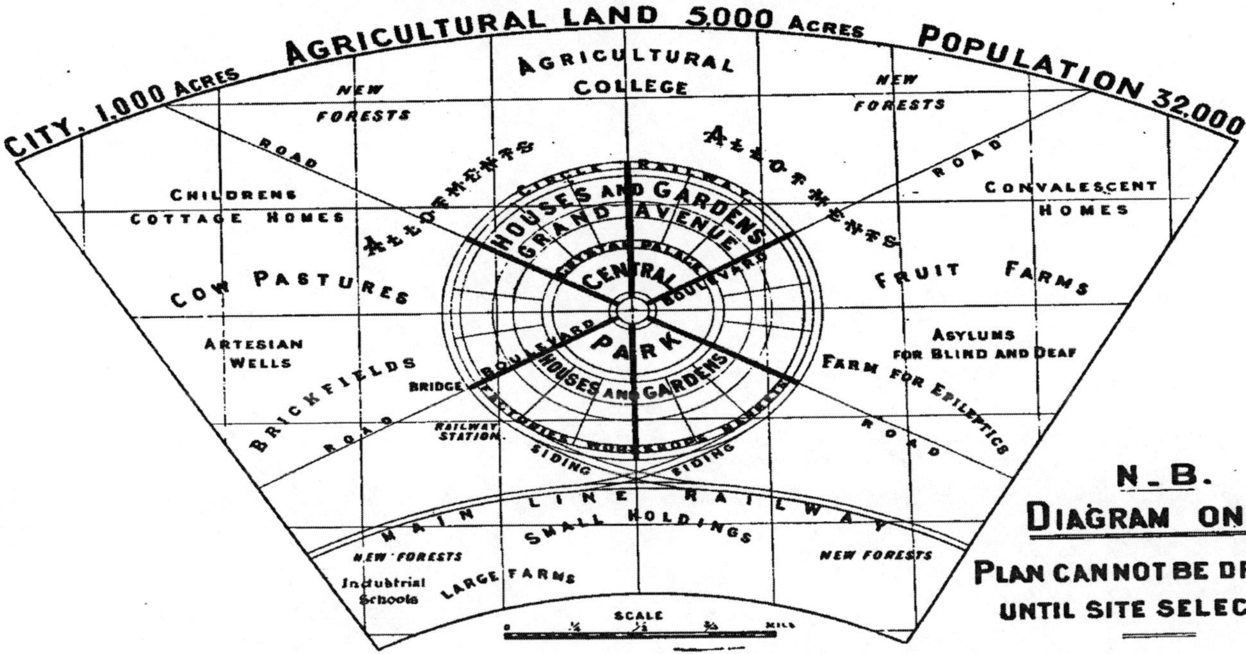

N. B.

DIAGRAM ONLY.

PLAN CANNOT BE DRAWN UNTIL SITE SELECTED

WARD AND CENTRE

GARDEN-CITY

No. 3.

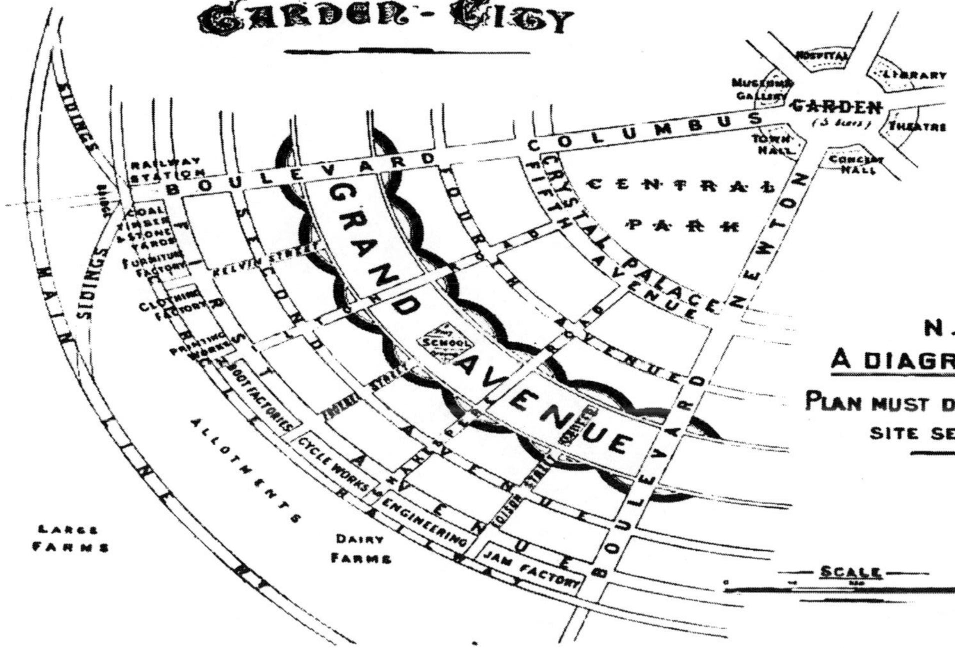

N.B.

A DIAGRAM ONLY.

PLAN MUST DEPEND UPON SITE SELECTED.

SCALE

is intersected by the boulevards) is a wide glass arcade called the "Crystal Palace," opening on to the park. This building is in wet weather one of the favourite resorts of the people, whilst the knowledge that its bright shelter is ever close at hand tempts people into Central Park, even in the most doubtful of weathers. Here manufactured goods are exposed for sale, and here most of that class of shopping which requires the joy of deliberation and selection is done. The space enclosed by the Crystal Palace is, however, a good deal larger than is required for these purposes, and a considerable part of it is used as a Winter Garden—the whole forming a permanent exhibition of a most attractive character, whilst its circular form brings it near to every dweller in the town—the furthest removed inhabitant being within 600 yards.

Passing out of the Crystal Palace on our way to the outer ring of the town, we cross Fifth Avenue—lined, as are all the roads of the town, with trees—fronting which, and looking on to the Crystal Palace, we find a ring of very excellently-built houses, each standing in its own ample grounds; and, as we continue our walk, we observe that the houses are for the most part built either in concentric rings, facing the various avenues (as the circular roads are termed), or fronting the boulevards and roads, which all converge to the centre of the town. Asking the friend who accompanies us on our journey what the population of this little city may be, we are told about 30,000 in the city itself, and about 2,000 in the agricultural estate, and that there are in the town 5,500 building lots of an *average* size of 20 feet × 130 feet—the minimum space allotted for the purpose being 20 × 100.

Noticing the very varied architecture and design which the houses and groups of houses display—some having common gardens and co-operative kitchens—we learn that general observance of street line or harmonious departure from it are the chief points as to house-building over which the municipal authorities exercise control, for, though proper sanitary arrangements are strictly enforced, the fullest measure of individual taste and preference is encouraged.

Walking still toward the outskirts of the town, we come upon "Grand Avenue." This avenue is fully entitled to the name it bears, for it is 420 feet wide,[1] and, forming a belt of green upwards of three miles long, divides that part of the town which lies outside Central Park into two belts. It really constitutes an additional park of 115 acres—a park which is within 240 yards of the furthest removed inhabitant. In this splendid avenue six sites, each of four acres, are occupied by public schools and their surrounding play-grounds and gardens, while other sites are reserved for churches, of such denominations as the religious beliefs of the people may determine, to be erected and maintained out of the funds of the worshippers and their friends. We observe that the houses fronting on Grand Avenue have departed (at least in one of the wards—that of which Diagram 3 is a representation)—from the general plan of concentric rings, and, in order to ensure a longer line of frontage on Grand Avenue, are arranged in crescents—thus also to the eye yet further enlarging the already splendid width of Grand Avenue.

[1] Portland Place, London, is only 100 feet wide.

On the outer ring of the town are factories, warehouses, dairies, markets, coal yards, timber yards, etc., all fronting on the circle railway, which encompasses the whole town, and which has sidings connecting it with a main line of railway which passes through the estate. This arrangement enables goods to be loaded direct into trucks from the warehouses and workshops, and so sent by railway to distant markets, or to be taken direct from the trucks into the warehouses or factories; thus not only effecting a very great saving in regard to packing and cartage, and reducing to a minimum loss from breakage, but also, by reducing the traffic on the roads of the town, lessening to a very marked extent the cost of their maintenance. The smoke fiend is kept well within bounds in Garden City; for all machinery is driven by electric energy, with the result that the cost of electricity for lighting and other purposes is greatly reduced.

The refuse of the town is utilised on the agricultural portions of the estate, which are held by various individuals in large farms, small holdings, allotments, cow pastures, etc.; the natural competition of these various methods of agriculture, tested by the willingness of occupiers to offer the highest rent to the municipality, tending to bring about the best system of husbandry, or, what is more probable, the best *systems* adapted for various purposes. Thus it is easily conceivable that it may prove advantageous to grow wheat in very large fields, involving united action under a capitalist farmer, or by a body of co-operators; while the cultivation of vegetables, fruits, and flowers, which requires closer and more personal care, and more of the artistic and inventive faculty, may possibly be best dealt with by individuals, or

3

by small groups of individuals having a common belief in the efficacy and value of certain dressings, methods of culture, or artificial and natural surroundings.

This plan, or, if the reader be pleased to so term it, this absence of plan, avoids the dangers of stagnation or dead level, and, though encouraging individual initiative, permits of the fullest co-operation, while the increased rents which follow from this form of competition are common or municipal property, and by far the larger part of them are expended in permanent improvements.

While the town proper, with its population engaged in various trades, callings, and professions, and with a store or depôt in each ward, offers the most natural market to the people engaged on the agricultural estate, inasmuch as to the extent to which the townspeople demand their produce they escape altogether any railway rates and charges; yet the farmers and others are not by any means limited to the town as their only market, but have the fullest right to dispose of their produce to whomsoever they please. Here, as in every feature of the experiment, it will be seen that it is not the area of rights which is contracted, but the area of choice which is enlarged.

This principle of freedom holds good with regard to manufacturers and others who have established themselves in the town. These manage their affairs in their own way, subject, of course, to the general law of the land, and subject to the provision of sufficient space for workmen and reasonable sanitary conditions. Even in regard to such matters as water, lighting, and telephonic communication—which a municipality, if efficient and honest, is certainly the best and most natural body to supply—no rigid or absolute monopoly is sought; and if any private corporation or any body of individuals proved itself capable of supplying on more advantageous terms, either the whole town or a section of it, with these or any commodities the supply of which was taken up by the corporation, this would be allowed. No really sound system of *action* is in more need of artificial support than is any sound system of *thought*. The area of municipal and corporate action is probably destined to become greatly enlarged; but, if it is to be so, it will be because the people possess faith in such action, and that faith can be best shown by a wide extension of the area of freedom.

Dotted about the estate are seen various charitable and philanthropic institutions. These are not under the control of the municipality, but are supported and managed by various public-spirited people who have been invited by the municipality to establish these institutions in an open healthy district, and on land let to them at a pepper-corn rent, it occurring to the authorities that they can the better afford to be thus generous, as the spending power of these institutions greatly benefits the whole community. Besides, as those persons who migrate to the town are among its most energetic and resourceful members, it is but just and right that their more helpless brethren should be able to enjoy the benefits of an experiment which is designed for humanity at large.

CHAPTER II.

THE REVENUE OF GARDEN CITY, AND HOW IT IS OBTAINED—THE AGRICULTURAL ESTATE.

AMONGST the essential differences between Garden City and other municipalities, one of the chief is its method of raising its revenue. Its entire revenue is derived from rents; and one of the purposes of this work is to show that the rents which may very reasonably be expected from the various tenants on the estate will be amply sufficient, if paid into the coffers of Garden City, (*a*) to pay the interest on the money with which the estate is purchased, (*b*) to provide a sinking-fund for the purpose of paying off the principal, (*c*) to construct and maintain all such works as are usually constructed and maintained by municipal and other local authorities out of rates compulsorily levied, and (*d*) (after redemption of debentures) to provide a large surplus for other purposes, such as old-age pensions or insurance against accident and sickness.

Perhaps no difference between town and country is more noticeable than the difference in the rent charged for the use of the soil. Thus, while in some parts of London the rent is equal to £30,000 an acre, £4 an acre is an extremely high rent for agricultural land. This enormous difference of rental value is, of course, almost entirely due to the presence in the one case and the absence in the other of a large population; and, as it cannot be attributed to the action of any particular individuals, it is frequently spoken of as the "unearned increment," *i.e.*, unearned by the landlord, though a more correct term would be "collectively-earned increment."

The presence of a considerable population thus giving a greatly additional value to the soil, it is obvious that a migration of population on any considerable scale to any particular area will be certainly attended with a corresponding rise in the value of the land so settled upon, and it is also obvious that such increment of value may, with some foresight and pre-arrangement, become the property of the migrating people.

Such foresight and pre-arrangement, never before exercised in an effective manner, are displayed conspicuously in the case of Garden City, where the land, as we have seen, is vested in trustees, who hold it in trust (after payment of the debentures) for the whole community, so that the entire increment of value gradually created becomes the property of the municipality, with the effect that though rents may rise, and even rise considerably, such rise in rent will not become the property of private individuals, but will be applied in relief of rates. It is this arrangement which will be seen to give Garden City much of its magnetic power.

The site of Garden City we have taken to be worth at the time of its purchase £40 an acre, or £240,000. The purchase money may be assumed to represent 30 years' purchase, and on this basis the annual rent paid by the former tenants was £8,000. If, therefore, there was a population of 1,000 persons upon the estate at the time of the purchase, then each man, woman, and child was contributing towards this rent-roll an average sum of £8 per annum. But the population of Garden City, including its agricultural land, is, when completed, 32,000, and the estate has cost them a sum on which they pay an annual charge by way of interest of £9,600. Thus, while before the experiment was initiated, 1,000 persons out of their united earnings contributed £8,000 a year, or *£8 a head*, on the completion of the town 32,000 persons out of their united earnings will contribute £9,600 a year, or an average of *6s. a head.*

This sum of 6s. per head per annum is all the rent, strictly speaking, which the inhabitants of Garden City will ever be called upon to pay; for it is all the rent which they *pay away*, any further sum they pay being a contribution towards their rates.

Let us now suppose that each person, besides contributing annually 6s. a head, contributes an average annual sum of £1 14s., or £2 in all. In that case two things may be noticed. First, each person will be paying for ground rent and rates only one-fourth of the sum which each person before the purchase paid in ground-rent alone; and, secondly, the Board of Management, after the payment of interest on the debentures, will receive an annual sum of £54,400, which, as will be presently shown, would, after providing a sinking fund (of £4,400), defray all those costs, charges, and expenses which are usually met by local taxation.

The average annual sum contributed by each man, woman, and child in England and Wales for local purposes is about £2 a head, and the average sum contributed for ground rent is, at a very low estimate, about £2 10s. The average yearly contribution for ground-rent and local rates is, therefore, about £4 10s. It might, therefore, be safely assumed that the people of Garden City would willingly pay £2 per head in complete discharge of ground-rent and local rates; but to make the case the clearer and stronger, we will test the supposed willingness of the tenants of Garden City to pay such a sum as £2 a year for rates and rents in another way.

For this purpose, let us deal first with the agricultural estate, leaving the town estate to be dealt with separately. Obviously the rent which can be secured will be considerably greater than before the town was built. Every farmer now has a market close to his doors. There are 30,000 townspeople to be fed. Those persons, of course, are perfectly free to get their food stuffs from any part of the world, and in the case of many products will doubtless continue to be supplied from abroad. These farmers are hardly likely to supply them with tea, with coffee, with spices, with tropical fruits or with sugar,[1] and their struggle to compete with America and Russia for the supply of wheat or flour to the town may be as keen as ever. But surely the struggle will not be so despairing. A ray—a beam of hope will gladden the heart of the despairing home-producer of wheat, for while the American has to pay railway charges to the sea-board, charges for Atlantic transit and railway charges to the consumer, the farmer of Garden City has a market at his very doors, and this a market which the rent he contributes will help to build up.[2]

[1] The electric light, with cheap motive power for its generation, with glass-houses, may make even some of these things possible.

[2] *See* "Fields, Farms, and Workshops," by Prince Krapotkin, 1/-, and "The Coming Revolution," by Capt. Petavel, 1/-, both published by Swan Sonnenschein & Co.

Or, consider vegetables and fruits. Farmers, except near towns, do not often grow them now. Why? Chiefly because of the difficulty and uncertainty of a market, and the high charges for freights and commission. To quote the words of Dr. Farquharson, M.P., when they "try to dispose of these things they find themselves struggling so hopelessly in a spider's web of rings, and middlemen, and speculators, that they are more than half-inclined to give up the attempt in despair, and fall back on those things that stand up straight and square to their prices in the open market." A curious calculation may be interesting with regard to milk. Assuming each person in the town consumed only one-third of a pint a day, then 30,000 would consume 1,250 gallons a day, and might thus save, taking railway charges at a penny per gallon, upwards of £1,900 per annum in railway rates upon the one item of milk, a saving which must be multiplied by a large figure in order to realise the general saving to be effected by placing consumer and producer in such close association. In other words, the combination of town and country is not only healthful, but economic—a point which every step taken will serve to make yet more clear.

But the rents which the agricultural tenants of Garden City would be willing to pay would increase for another reason. The waste products of the town could, and this without heavy charges for railway transport or other expensive agencies, be readily brought back to the soil, thus increasing its fertility. The question of sewage disposal is naturally a difficult one to deal with, but its inherent difficulty is often much increased by artificial and imperfect conditions already in existence. Thus, Sir Benjamin Baker, in his joint report with Mr. (now Sir)

Alexander Binnie to the London County Council, says: "In approaching the consideration of the vast question of the whole sewerage system of the Metropolis, and the state of the Thames, as a practical problem . . . we had clearly at once to recognise the fact that the general features of the main drainage system were unalterably settled, and must be accepted in the same way as the main lines of thoroughfares have to be accepted whether quite as we could wish them to be or not." But on Garden City site, given the skilful engineer, he would have comparatively little difficulty. He would have, as it were, a clean sheet on which to prepare his plans, and the whole estate being equally the property of the municipality, he would have a free course before him, and would doubtless succeed in adding greatly to the productiveness of the agricultural estate.

The great increase in the number of allotments, especially such favourably situated allotments as are shown in Diagram 2, would also tend to raise the total sum offered in rent.

There are yet other reasons why the rent which a farmer on the Garden City estate would be willing to pay for his farm, or a labourer for his allotment, would tend to increase. The productiveness of the agricultural part of the estate, besides being increased by a well-devised system of sewage disposal, and by a new and somewhat extensive market, with unique conveniences for transit to more distant markets, would also be increased because the tenure on which the land is held encourages maximum cultivation. It is a just tenure. The agricultural portion of the estate is let at fair rents, with a right to continue in occupation as long as the tenant is willing to pay a rent equal to that offered by any would-be occupier, less, say, 10 per cent. in favour of the occupying tenant—the incoming tenant having also to compensate the outgoing tenant for all unexhausted improvements. Under this system, while it would be impossible for the tenant to secure to himself any undue share of that natural increment of land-value which would be brought about by the general growth in well-being of the town, he would yet have, as all tenants in possession probably should have, a preference over any new-comer, and would know that he would not lose those fruits of his past industry which were not yet ingathered but were still adding their value to the soil. Surely no one can doubt that such a tenure would, of itself, tend greatly to increase at once the activity and industry of the tenant, the productivity of the soil, and the rent which the tenant would be willing to pay.

That there would be this increased offer of rent will become yet more obvious if we consider for a moment the *nature* of the rent paid by a tenant of Garden City. Part of what he pays would be in respect of interest on the debentures on which the money to purchase the estate was raised, or in the redemption of those debentures, and would thus, except so far as the debentures were held by residents on the estate, pass away from the community altogether; but the whole of the remaining sum paid would be expended locally, and the farmer would have a share equal to that of every adult in the administration of such money. The term "rent," therefore, has, in Garden City, acquired a new meaning, and, for the sake of clearness, it will be necessary in future to use terms which will not be ambiguous. That part of the rent which represents interest on debentures will be hereafter called "landlord's rent"; that part which represents repayment of purchase-money "sinking fund"; that part which is devoted to public purposes "rates"; while the total sum will be termed "rate-rent."

From these considerations, surely it is obvious that the "*rate-rent*" which the farmer will be willing to pay into the treasury of Garden City will be considerably higher than the *rent* he would be willing to pay to a private landlord, who, besides increasing his rent as the farmer makes his land more valuable, will also leave him with the full burden of local taxation resting upon him. In short the plan proposed embraces a system of sewage-disposal which will return to the soil in a transmuted form many of those products the growth of which, by exhausting its natural fertility, demand elsewhere the application of manures so expensive that the farmer becomes sometimes blinded to their necessity, and it also embraces a system of rate-rents by which many of the farmer's hard-earned sovereigns, hitherto lost to him by being paid away to his landlord, shall return to his exhausted exchequer, not indeed in the form in which they left it, but in a variety of useful forms, such as roads, schools, markets, which will assist him most materially, though indirectly, in his work, but which, under present conditions, entail so severe a burden as to make him naturally slow to see their inherent necessity, and even to look upon some of them with suspicion and dislike. Who can doubt that if the farm and the farmer can be placed under conditions so healthful and natural alike in a physical and moral sense, the willing soil and the hopeful farmer will alike respond to their new environment—the soil becoming more fertile by every blade of grass it yields, the farmer richer by every penny of rate-rent he contributes?

We are now in a position to see that the rate-rent which will be readily paid by farmer, small occupier, and allotment holder, would be considerably greater than the rent he paid before (1) because of the presence of a new town population demanding new and more profitable farm products, in respect of which railway charges can be largely saved; (2) by the due return to the soil of its natural elements; (3) by the just, equitable, and natural conditions on which the land is held; and (4) by reason of the fact that the rent now paid is *rate and rent*, while the rent formerly paid left the rates to be paid by the tenant.

But certain as it is that the "*rate-rent*" would represent a very considerable increase over the bare *rent* formerly paid by the tenants on the estate, it is still very much a matter of conjecture what the "rate-rent" would be; and we shall, therefore, be acting prudently if we greatly under-estimate the "rate-rent" which would probably be offered. If, then, in view of all the circumstances, we estimate that the *farming population* of Garden City will be prepared to pay for rates and rent 50 per cent. more than they before paid for *rent alone*, we shall reach the following result:—

Estimated Gross Revenue from Agricultural Estate.

Original rent paid by tenants of 5,000 acres, say	£6,500
Add 50 per cent. for contributions to rates and sinking fund, - - - - - - -	3,250
Total "rate-rent" from agricultural estate, - - - - - -	£9,750

We shall in the next chapter estimate the amount which may, on the most reasonable calculation, be expected from the town estate, and then proceed to consider the sufficiency of the total rate-rents for the municipal needs of the town.

CHAPTER III.

THE REVENUE OF GARDEN CITY—TOWN ESTATE.

"Whatever reforms be introduced into the dwellings of the London poor, it will still remain true that the whole area of London is insufficient to supply its population with fresh air and the free space that is wanted for wholesome recreation. A remedy for the overcrowding of London will still be wanted. . . . There are large classes of the population of London whose removal into the country would be in the long run economically advantageous; it would benefit alike those who moved and those who remained behind. . . . Of the 150,000 or more hired workers in the clothes-making trades, by far the greater part are very poorly paid, and do work which it is against all economic reason to have done where ground-rent is high."—Professor Marshall, "The Housing of the London Poor," *Contemporary Review*, 1884.

HAVING in the last chapter estimated the gross revenue which may be anticipated from the agricultural part of the estate at £9,750, we will now turn to the town estate (where, obviously, the conversion of an agricultural area into a town will be attended with a very large rise in land values), and endeavour roughly to estimate—again taking care to keep well within the mark—the amount of "rate-rent" which will be freely offered by the tenants of the town estate.

The site of the town proper consists, it will be remembered, of 1,000 acres, and is assumed to have cost £40,000, the interest of which, at 4 per cent., is £1,600 per annum. This sum of £1,600 is, therefore, all the landlord's rent which the people of the town site will be called upon to pay, any additional "rate-rent" they may contribute being devoted either to the payment of the purchase-money as "sinking-fund," or applied as "rates" to the construction and maintenance of roads, schools, water-works, and to other municipal purposes. It will be interesting, therefore, to see what sort of a burden "landlord's rent" will represent per head, and what the community would secure by such contribution. Now, if the sum of £1,600, being the annual interest or "landlord's rent," be divided by 30,000 (the supposed population of the town), it will be found to equal an annual contribution by each man, woman, and child of *rather less than 1s. 1d. per head.* This is all the "landlord's rent" which will ever be levied, any additional sum collected as "rate-rent" being applied to sinking-fund or to local purposes.

And now let us notice what this fortunately-placed community obtains for this insignificant sum. It obtains for 1s. 1d. per head per annum, first, ample sites for homes, these averaging, as we have seen, 20 feet by 130 feet, and accommodating, on an average, 5½ persons to each lot. It obtains ample space for roads, some of which are of truly magnificent proportions, so wide and spacious that sunlight and air may freely circulate, and in which trees, shrubs, and grass give to the town a semi-rural appearance. It also obtains ample sites for town-hall, public library, museum and picture-gallery, theatre, concert-hall, hospital, schools, churches, swimming baths, public markets, etc. It also secures a central park of 145 acres, and a magnificent avenue 420 feet wide, extending in a circle of over three miles, unbroken save by spacious boulevards and by schools and churches, which, one may be sure, will not be the less beautiful because so little money has been expended on their sites.

It secures also all the land required for a railway 4¼ miles long, encompassing the town; 82 acres for warehouses, factories, markets, and a splendid site for a crystal palace devoted to shopping, and serving also as a winter garden.

The leases under which all building sites are let do not, therefore, contain the usual covenant by the tenant to pay all rates, taxes, and assessments levied in respect of such property, but, on the contrary, contain a covenant by the landlord to apply the whole sum received, first, in payment of debenture interest; secondly, towards the redemption of the debentures; and thirdly, as to the whole of the balance, into a public fund, to be applied to public purposes, among these being the rates levied by public authorities, other than the municipal authority, of the city.[1]

Let us now attempt to estimate the rate-rents which may be anticipated in respect of our town-estate.

First, we will deal with the home-building lots. All are excellently situated, but those fronting Grand Avenue (420 feet) and the magnificent boulevards (120 feet) would probably call forth the highest tenders. We can here deal only with averages, but we think anyone would admit that an average rate-rent of 6s. a foot frontage for home lots would be extremely moderate. *This would make the rate-rent of a building lot* 20 *feet wide in an average position* £6 *a year, and on this basis the* 5,500 *building lots would yield a gross revenue of* £33,000.

The rate-rents from the sites of factories, warehouses,

[1] The question of the form of Leases to be granted is one which is being carefully considered by the Land Tenure Section of the Garden City Association.

markets, etc., cannot perhaps be so well estimated by the foot frontage, but we may perhaps safely assume that an average employer would willingly pay £2 in respect of each employee. It is, of course, not suggested that the rate-rent levied should be a poll-tax; it would, as has been said, be raised by competition among the tenants; but this way of estimating rate-rent to be paid will perhaps give a ready means by which manufacturers or other employers, co-operative societies, or individuals working on their own account, would be able to judge whether they would be lightly rated and rented as compared with their present position. It must be, however, distinctly borne in mind that we are dealing with *averages;* and if the figure should seem high to a large employer, it will seem ridiculously low to a small shopkeeper.

Now, in a town with a population of 30,000, there would be about twenty thousand persons between the ages of 16 and 65; and if it is assumed that 10,625 of these would be employed in factories, shops, warehouses, markets, etc., or in any way which involved the use of a site, other than a home-building site, to be leased from the municipality, there would be a revenue from this source of £21,250.

The gross revenue of the entire estate would therefore be:—

Rate-rent from agricultural estate (*see* p. 36), -	£9,750
,, 5,500 home building lots at £6 per lot, - - - - - - -	33,000
,, from business premises 10,625 persons employed at an average of £2 a head,	21,250
	£64,000

Or £2 per head of population for rates and rent.

This sum would be available as follows:—

For landlord's rent or interest on purchase money £240,000 at 4 per cent., - - -	£9,600
For sinking fund (30 years), - - - -	4,400
For such purposes as are elsewhere defrayed out of rates, - - - - - -	50,000
	£64,000

It is now important to inquire whether £50,000 will suffice for the municipal needs of Garden City.

CHAPTER IV.

THE REVENUE OF GARDEN CITY—GENERAL OBSERVATIONS ON ITS EXPENDITURE.

Before entering upon the question which presented itself at the conclusion of the last chapter—that of endeavouring to ascertain whether the estimated net available income of Garden City (£50,000 per annum) would be sufficient for its municipal needs, I will very shortly state how it is proposed to raise the money required for commencing operations. The money would be borrowed on "B" debentures,[1] and would be secured by a charge upon the "rate-rent," subject, of course, to the payment of interest and sinking fund in respect of the "A" debentures on which the purchase money of the estate is raised. It is, perhaps, superfluous to remark that, though in the case of the land purchase it might be requisite to raise the whole, or at least some very considerable part of the purchase money before possession would be given of the estate, or operations upon it commenced, yet in regard to public works to be carried out upon the estate, the case is quite different, and it would be by no means necessary or advisable to defer the commencement of operations until the whole sum which might be ultimately required should be raised. Probably no town was ever built on such onerous conditions as would be involved in the

[1] *See* note on page 21.

raising at the outset of such a very considerable sum as would defray the cost of all its public works; and though the circumstances under which Garden City is to be built may be unique, there is, as will by and by be seen, not only no need for making an exception of the town in respect of initial capital, but quite exceptional reasons will become more and more apparent which make the overlaying of the enterprise with superabundant capital altogether unnecessary, and therefore inexpedient; although, of course, there must be a sufficient sum to enable all real economies to be readily effected.

Perhaps it may be well in this connection to draw a distinction as to the amount of capital required between the case of the building of a town and the building, let us say, of a large iron bridge across an estuary. In the case of the bridge it is highly expedient to raise the entire sum required before commencing operations, for the simple reason that the bridge is not a bridge until the last rivet is driven home, nor, until its entire completion and its connection with the railways or roadways at either end, has it any revenue-earning power. Except, therefore, on the assumption that it is to be fully completed, it offers very little security for the capital sunk upon it. Hence it would be very natural for those who are asked to invest to say, "We will not put any money into this enterprise until you show us that you can get enough to complete it." But the money which it is proposed to raise for the development of Garden City site leads to speedy results. It is to be expended upon roads, schools, etc. These works will be carried out with due regard to the number of lots which have been let to tenants, who undertake to build as from a certain date; and, therefore, the money expended will very soon begin to yield a return in the shape of a rate-rent, representing, in reality, a greatly-improved ground-rent; when those who have advanced money on the "B" debentures will have a really first-class security, and further sums should be easily obtainable, and at a reduced rate of interest. Again, it is an important part of the project that each ward, or one-sixth part of the city, should be in some sense a complete town by itself, and thus the school buildings might serve, in the earlier stages, not only as schools, but as places for religious worship, for concerts, for libraries, and for meetings of various kinds, so that all outlay on expensive municipal and other buildings might be deferred until the later stages of the enterprise. Work, too, would be practically completed in one ward before commencing on another, and the operations in the various wards would be taken up in due and proper sequence, so that those portions of the town site on which building operations were not in progress would also be a source of revenue, either as allotments, cow-pastures, or, perhaps, as brickfields.

Let us now deal with the subject immediately before us. Will the principles on which Garden City is to be built have any bearing on the effectiveness of its municipal expenditure? In other words, will a given revenue yield greater results than under ordinary conditions? These questions will be answered in the affirmative. It will be shown that, pound for pound, money will be more effectively spent than elsewhere, and that there will be many great and obvious economies which cannot be expressed in figures with much accuracy, but which would certainly represent in the aggregate a very large sum.

The first great economy to be noticed is that the item of "landlord's rent," which, under ordinary conditions, largely enters into municipal expenditure, will, in Garden City, scarcely enter at all. Thus, all well-ordered towns require administrative buildings, schools, swimming baths, libraries, parks; and the sites which these and other corporate undertakings occupy are usually purchased. In such cases the money necessary for the purchase of the sites is generally borrowed on the security of the rates; and thus it is that a very considerable part of the total rates levied by a municipality are ordinarily applied, not to productive works, but either to what we have termed "landlord's rent," in the shape of interest on money borrowed to effect the purchase, or to the provision of a sinking fund in payment of the purchase money of the land so acquired, which is landlord's rent in a capitalised form.

Now, in Garden City, all such expenditure, with such exceptions as road sites on the agricultural estate, has been already provided for. Thus, the 250 acres for public parks, the sites for schools and other public buildings, will cost the ratepayers nothing whatever, or, to put it more correctly, their cost, which was really £40 per acre, has been covered, as we have seen, by the annual average contribution of 1s. 1d. per head, which each person is supposed to make in discharge of landlord's rent; and the revenue of the town, £50,000, is the *net* revenue after all interest and sinking fund in respect of the whole site has been deducted. In considering, therefore, the question whether £50,000 is a sufficient revenue, it must be remembered that in no case has any cost of municipal sites to be first deducted from that amount.

Another item in which a great economy will be effected will be found in a comparison between Garden City and any old city like London. London wishes to breathe a fuller municipal spirit, and so proceeds to construct schools, to pull down slums, to erect libraries, swimming baths, etc. In these cases, it has not only to purchase the freeholds of the sites, but also has usually to pay for the buildings which had been previously erected thereon, and which are purchased solely, of course, with a view to their demolition and to a clearing of the ground, and frequently it has also to meet claims for business-disturbance, together with heavy legal expenses in settling claims. In this connection it may be remarked that the inclusive cost of *sites* of schools purchased by the London School Board since its constitution, *i.e.*, the cost, including old buildings, business-disturbance, law charges, etc., has already reached the enormous sum of £3,516,072,[1] and the exclusive cost of the sites (370 acres in extent) ready for building by the Board is equal, on the average, to £9,500 per acre.

At this rate the cost of the 24 acres of school sites for Garden City would be £228,000, so that another site for a model city could be purchased out of what would be saved in Garden City in respect of school sites alone. "Oh, but," it may be said, "the school sites of Garden City are extravagantly large, and would be out of the question in London, and it is altogether unfair to compare a small town like Garden City with London, the wealthy capital of a mighty Empire." I would reply, "It is quite true that the cost of land in London would

[1] See Report, London School Board, 6th May, 1897, p. 1480.

make such sites extravagant, not to say prohibitive—they would cost about £40,000,000 sterling—but does not this of itself suggest a most serious defect of system, and that at a most vital part? Can children be better taught where land costs £9,500 an acre than where it costs £40? Whatever may be the real economic value of the London site, for other purposes—as to which we may have something to say at a later stage—for school purposes, wherein lies the advantage that the sites on which its schools are built are frequently surrounded by dingy factories or crowded courts and alleys? If Lombard Street is an ideal place for banks, is not a park like the Central Avenue of Garden City an ideal place for schools?—and is not the welfare of our children the primary consideration with any well-ordered community?" "But," it may be said, "the children must be educated near their homes, and these homes must be near the places where their parents work." Precisely; but does not the scheme provide for this in the most effective manner, and in that respect also are not the school sites of Garden City superior to those of London? The children will have to expend less than an average amount of energy in going to school, a matter, as all educationists admit, of immense importance, especially in the winter. But further, have we not heard from Professor Marshall (see heading to Chapter III.) that "150,000 people, in London, engaged in the clothes-making trades, are doing work which it is against all economic reason to have done where ground-rent is high"—in other words, that these 150,000 people *should not be in London at all;* and does not the consideration that the education of the children of such workers is carried on at once under inferior conditions and at enormous cost add weight and significance to the Professor's words? If these workers ought not to be in London, then their homes, for which, insanitary as they are, they pay heavy rents, ought not to be in London; a certain proportion of the shop-keepers who supply their wants should not be in London; and various other people to whom the wages earned by these persons in the clothes-making trade give employment should not be in London. Hence, there is a sense—and a very real one—in which it *is* fair to compare the cost of school sites in Garden City with the cost of school sites in London; because obviously if these people do, as suggested by Professor Marshall, migrate from London, they can at once effect (if they make, as I have suggested, proper provision beforehand) not only a great saving in respect of ground-rent for their workshops, but also a vast saving in respect of sites for homes, schools, and other purposes; and this saving is obviously the difference between what is now paid and what would be paid under the new conditions, minus the loss incurred (if any), and plus the numerous gains secured as the result of such removal.

Let us for the sake of clearness make the comparison in another way. The people of London have paid a capital sum representing, when spread over the whole population of London (this being taken at 6,000,000), upwards of 11s. 6d. per head of population for school sites held by the London School Board, a sum which is, of course, exclusive of the sites for voluntary schools. The population of Garden City, 30,000 in number, have entirely saved that 11s. 6d. per head, making a total saving of £17,250, which at 3 per cent. involves an annual saving of £517 in perpetuity. And besides thus saving £517 a year as interest on cost of sites for schools, Garden City has secured sites for its schools incomparably better than those of London schools—sites which afford ample accommodation for all the children of the town, and not, as in the case of the London School Board, accommodation for only half of the children of the municipality. (The sites of the London School Board are 370 acres in extent, or about 1 acre to every 16,000 of the population, while the people of Garden City have obtained 24 acres or 1 acre for every 1,250.) In other words, Garden City secures sites which are larger, better placed, and in every way more suitable for educational purposes, at a mere fraction of the cost which in London is incurred for sites vastly inferior in every respect.

The economies with which we have thus dealt are, it will be seen, effected by the two simple expedients we have referred to. First, by buying the land *before* a new value is given to it by migration, the migrating people obtain a site at an extremely low figure, and secure the coming increment for themselves and those who come after them; and secondly, by coming to a new site, they do not have to pay large sums for old buildings, for compensation for disturbance, and for heavy legal charges. The practicability of securing for the poor workers of London the first of these great advantages appears to have been for the moment overlooked by Professor Marshall in his article in the *Contemporary Review*,[1] for the Professor remarks "Ultimately all would gain by the migration, *but most*" (the italics are

[1] No one is, of course, better aware of this possibility than the Professor himself. (*See* "Principles of Economics," (2nd ed.) Book v., Chap. x. and xiii.)

my own) "*the landowners and the railroads connected with the colony.*" Let us then adopt the expedient here advocated of securing that the *landowners*, "*who . . . will gain most*" by a project specially designed to benefit a class now low down in the social scale, *shall be those very people themselves*, as members of a new municipality, and then a strong additional inducement will be held out to them to make a change, which nothing but the lack of combined effort has hitherto prevented. As to the benefit to be derived by the railways, while no doubt the building up of the town would specially benefit the main line of railway which passed through the estate, it is also true that the earnings of the people would not be diminished to the usual extent by railway freights and charges. (*See* Chap. ii., also Chap. v., page 60.)

We now come to deal with an element of economy which will be simply incalculable. This is to be found in the fact that the town is definitely planned, so that the whole question of municipal administration may be dealt with by one far-reaching scheme. It is not by any means necessary, and it is not, humanly speaking, possible, that the final scheme should be the work of one mind. It will no doubt be the work of many minds—the minds of engineers, of architects and surveyors, of landscape gardeners and electricians. But it is essential, as we have said, that there should be unity of design and purpose—that the town should be planned as a whole, and not left to grow up in a chaotic manner as has been the case with all English towns, and more or less so with the towns of all countries. A town, like a flower, or a tree, or an animal, should, at each stage of its growth, possess unity, symmetry, completeness, and the effect of growth should never be to destroy that unity, but to give it greater purpose, nor to mar that symmetry, but to make it more symmetrical; while the completeness of the early structure should be merged in the yet greater completeness of the later development.

Garden City is not only planned, but it is planned with a view to the very latest of modern requirements;[1] and it is obviously always easier, and usually far more economical and completely satisfactory, to make out of fresh material a new instrument than to patch up and alter an old one. This element of economy will be perhaps best dealt with by a concrete illustration, and one of a very striking nature at once presents itself.

In London the question of building a new street between Holborn and the Strand has been for many years under consideration, and at length a scheme is being carried out, imposing an enormous cost on the

[1] "London has grown up in a chaotic manner, without any unity of design, and at the chance discretion of any persons who were fortunate enough to own land as it came into demand at successive periods for building operations. Sometimes a great landlord laid out a quarter in a manner to tempt the better class of residents by squares, gardens, or retired streets, often cut off from through traffic by gates and bars; but even in these cases London as a whole has not been thought of, and no main arteries have been provided for. In other and more frequent cases of small landowners, the only design of builders has been to crowd upon the land as many streets and houses as possible, regardless of anything around them, and without open spaces or wide approaches. A careful examination of a map of London shows how absolutely wanting in any kind of plan has been its growth, and how little the convenience and wants of the whole population or the considerations of dignity and beauty have been consulted."—Right Hon. G. J. Shaw-Lefevre, *New Review*, 1891, p. 435.

people of London. "Every such change in the street geography of London displaces thousands of the poor"—I quote from the *Daily Chronicle* of July 6, 1898—"and for many years all public or quasi-public schemes have been charged with the liability to re-house as many of them as possible. This is as it should be; but the difficulty begins when the public is asked to face the music and pay the bill. In the present case some three thousand souls of the working population have to be turned out. After some searching of heart, it is decided that most of them are so closely tied to the spot by their employment that it would be a hardship to send them more than a mile away. The result, in cash, is that London must spend in re-housing them about £100 a head—or £300,000 in all. As to those who cannot fairly be asked to go even a mile away—hangers-on to the market, or others tethered to the spot—the cost will be even higher. They will require to have parcels of the precious land cleared by the great scheme itself, and the result of that will be to house them at the handsome figure of £260 a-piece, or some £1,400 for every family of five or six. Financial statements convey little to the ordinary mind. Let us make it a little more intelligible. A sum of £1,400 means, in the house market, a rental of nearly £100 a year. It would buy an excellent, in fact a sumptuous, house and garden at Hampstead, such as the better middle-class delight in. It would purchase anywhere in the nearer suburbs such houses as men with £1,000 a year inhabit. If one went further afield, to the new neighbourhoods which the City clerk can easily reach by rail, a £1,400 house represents actual magnificence." But on what scale of comfort will the poor Covent Garden labourer with a wife and four children live? The £1,400 will by no means represent a fair standard of comfort, to say nothing of magnificence. "He will live in three rooms sufficiently small in a block at least three storeys high." Contrast this with what might be done on a new area, by carefully planning a bold scheme at the outset. Streets of greater width than this new street would be laid out and constructed at a mere fraction of the cost, while a sum of £1,400, instead of providing 1 family with "three rooms sufficiently small in blocks at least three storeys high," would provide 7 families in Garden City with a comfortable six-roomed cottage each, and with a nice little garden; and, manufacturers being concurrently induced to build on the sites set apart for them, each breadwinner would be placed within easy walking distance of his work.

There is another modern need which all towns and cities should be designed to meet—a need which has arisen with the evolution of modern sanitation, and which has of recent years been accentuated by the rapid growth of invention. Subways for sewerage and surface drainage, for water, gas, telegraph and telephone wires, electric lighting wires, wires for conveying motive power, pneumatic tubes for postal purposes, have come to be regarded as economic if not essential. But if they would be a source of economy in an old city, how much more so in new ones; for on a clean sheet it will be easy to use the very best appliances for their construction, and to avail ourselves to the fullest extent of the ever-growing advantages which they possess as the number of services which they accommodate increases. Before the subways can be constructed, trenches somewhat wide and deep must be excavated. In making these the most approved excavating machinery could be employed. In old towns this might be very objectionable, if not, indeed, quite impossible. But here, in Garden City, the steam navvy would not make its appearance in the parts where people were living, but where they were coming to live after its work in preparing the way had been completed. What a grand thing it would be if the people of England could, by an actual illustration under their very eyes, be convinced that machinery can be so used as to confer not only an ultimate national benefit, but a direct and immediate advantage, and that not only upon those who actually own it or use it, but on others who are given work by its magic aid. What a happy day it would be for the people of this country, and of all countries, if they could learn, from practical experience, that machinery can be used on an extended scale to *give* employment as well as *to take it away*—to *implace* labour as well as to *displace* it—to free men as well as to *enslave* them. There will be plenty of work to be done in Garden City. That is obvious. It is also obvious that, until a large number of houses and factories are built, many of these things cannot be done, and that the faster the trenches are dug, the subways finished, the factories and the houses built, and the light and the power turned on, the sooner can this town, the home of an industrious and a happy people, be built, and the sooner can others start the work of building other towns, not like it, but gradually becoming as much superior to it as our present locomotives are to the first crude attempts of the pioneers of mechanical traction.

We have now shown four cogent reasons why a given

revenue should, in Garden City, yield vastly greater results than under ordinary conditions.

(1) That no "landlord's rent" or interest in respect of freeholds would be payable other than the small amount which has been already provided for in estimating net revenue.

(2) That the site being practically clear of buildings and other works, but little expenditure would be incurred in the purchase of such buildings, or compensation for business-disturbance, or legal and other expenses in connection therewith.

(3) The economy arising out of a definite plan, and one in accordance with modern needs and requirements, thus saving those items of expenditure which are incurred in old cities as it is sought to bring them into harmony with modern ideas.

(4) The possibility, as the whole site will be clear for operations, of introducing machinery of the very best and most modern type in road-making and other engineering operations.

There are other economies which will become apparent to the reader as he proceeds, but, having cleared the ground by discussing general principles, we shall be better prepared to discuss the question as to the sufficiency of our estimates in another chapter.

CHAPTER V.

FURTHER DETAILS OF EXPENDITURE ON GARDEN CITY.

To make this chapter interesting to the general reader would be difficult, perhaps impossible; but if carefully studied, it will, I think, be found to abundantly establish one of the main propositions of this book—that the rate-rent of a well-planned town, built on an agricultural estate, will amply suffice for the creation and maintenance of such municipal undertakings as are usually provided for out of rates compulsorily levied.

The net available revenue of Garden City, after payment of interest on debentures and providing a sinking fund for the landed estate, has been already estimated at £50,000 per annum (see Chap. iii., page 42). Having, in the fourth chapter, given special reasons why a given expenditure in Garden City would be unusually productive, I will now enter into fuller details, so that any criticism which this book may elicit, having something tangible to deal with, may be the more valuable in preparing the ground for an experiment such as is here advocated.

	Expenditure.	
	On Capital Account.	On Maintenance and Working Expenses.
(See Note A) 25 Miles road (city) at £4,000 a mile	£100,000	£2,500
(,, B) 6 Miles additional roads, country estate at £1,200	7,200	350
(,, C) Circular railway and bridges, 5½ miles at £3,000	16,500	1,500 (maintenance only)
(,, D) Schools for 6,400 children, or ⅕ of the total population, at £12 per school place for capital account, and £3 maintenance, etc.	76,800	19,200
(,, E) Town Hall	10,000	2,000
(,, F) Library	10,000	600
(,, G) Museum...	10,000	600
(,, H) Parks, 250 acres at £50	12,500	1,250
(,, I) Sewage disposal ...	20,000	1,000
	£263,000	£29,000
(,, K) Interest on £263,000 at 4½ per cent.		11,835
(,, L) Sinking Fund to provide for extinction of debt in 30 years		4,480
(,, M) Balance available for rates levied by local bodies within the area of which the estate is situated		4,685
		£50,000

Besides the above expenditure, a considerable outlay would be incurred in respect of markets, water supply, lighting, tramways, and other revenue-yielding undertakings. But these items of expenditure are almost invariably attended with considerable profits, which go in aid of rates. No calculation, therefore, need be made in respect of these.

I will now deal separately with most of the items in the above estimate.

A. Roads and Streets.

The first point to be observed under this head is that the cost of making new streets to meet the growth of population is generally not borne by the ground landlord nor defrayed out of the rates. It is usually paid by the building-owner before the local authorities will consent to take the road over as a free gift. It is obvious, therefore, that the greater part of the £100,000 *might* be struck out. Experts will also not forget that the cost of the road sites is elsewhere provided for. In considering the question of the actual sufficiency of the estimate, they will also remember that of the boulevards one-half and of the streets and avenues one-third may be regarded as in the nature of park, and the cost of laying out and maintenance of these portions of the roads is dealt with under the head "Parks." They will also note that road-making materials would probably be found near at hand, and that, the railway relieving the streets of most of the heavy traffic, the more expensive methods of paving need not be resorted to. The cost, £4,000 per mile, would, however, be doubtless inadequate if subways are constructed, as probably they ought to be. The following consideration, however, has led me not to estimate for these. Subways are, where useful, a source of economy. The cost of maintaining roads is lessened, as the continual breaking-up for laying and repairing of water, gas, and electric mains is avoided, while any waste from leaky pipes is quickly detected, and thus the subways *pay*. Their cost should, therefore, be debited rather to cost of water, gas, and electric supplies, and these services are almost invariably a source of revenue to the Company or Corporation which constructs them.

B. Country Roads.

These roads are only 40 feet wide, and £1,200 a mile is ample. The cost of sites has in this case to be defrayed out of estimate.

C. Circular Railway and Bridges.

The cost of site is elsewhere provided for (*see* p. 40). The cost of maintenance does not, of course, include working expenses, locomotives, etc. To cover these a charge based on cost might be made to traders using the line. It should also be noticed that, as in the case of roads, by showing that the expense of this undertaking could be defrayed out of the rate-rent, I am proving more than I undertook to prove. I am proving that the rate-rent is sufficient to provide for landlords' rent, for such purposes as are usually defrayed out of rent, *and also for greatly extending the area of municipal activity.*

It may here be well to point out that this circle railway not only will save the trader the expense of carting to and from his warehouse or factory, but will enable him to claim a rebate from the railway company. Section 4 of the Railway and Canal Tariff Act, 1894, enacts: "Whenever merchandise is received or delivered by a railway company at any siding or branch railway not belonging to the company, and a dispute arises between the railway company and the consignor or consignee of such merchandise, as to any allowance or rebate from the rates charged to such consignor or consignee, in respect that the railway company does not provide station accommodation or perform terminal services, the Railway and Canal Commissioners shall have jurisdiction to hear and determine what, if any, is a just and reasonable allowance or rebate."

D. Schools.

This estimate of £12 per school place represents what was only a few years ago (1892) the average cost per child of the London School Board for building, architect, and clerk of the works, and for furniture and fittings; and no one can doubt that buildings greatly superior to those in London could be obtained for this sum. The saving in sites has been already dealt with, but it may be remarked that in London the cost per child for sites has been £6 11s 10d.

As showing how ample this estimate is, it may be observed that the cost of schools which have been proposed to be built by a private company at Eastbourne, "with a view of keeping out the School Board," is estimated at £2,500 for 400 places, or but little more than half the sum per school place provided in the estimate for Garden City.

The cost of maintenance, £3 per head, is probably sufficient, in view of the fact that the "expenditure per scholar in actual average attendance" in England and Wales, as given in the Report of the Committee of Council on Education, 1896-97, c. 8545, is £2 11s. 11½d. It must be especially noticed, too, that the whole cost of education is, in these estimates, assumed to be borne by Garden City, though a considerable part would be, in the ordinary course, borne by the National Exchequer. The amount of income per scholar in actual average attendance in England and Wales, as given in the same report, is £1 1s. 2d. as against a rate in Garden City of £3. So that I am again, in the case of the schools, as in the case of roads and circle railway, proving more than I set out to prove.

E. Town Hall and Expenses of Management.

It is to be noticed that the estimates of the various undertakings are intended to cover professional direction and supervision of architects, engineers, teachers, etc. The £2,000 for maintenance and working expenses under this head is, therefore, intended to include only the salaries of town clerk and of officials other than those comprised under special heads, together with incidental expenses.

F. Library, and G. Museum.

The latter is usually and the former not infrequently elsewhere provided for out of funds other than rates. So, here again, I am more than proving my case.

H. Parks and Road Ornamentation.

This item of cost would not be incurred until the undertaking was in a thoroughly sound financial condition, and the park space for a considerable period might be a source of revenue as agricultural land. Further, much of the park space would probably be left in a state of nature. Forty acres of this park space is road ornamentation, but the planting of trees and shrubs would not entail great expense. Again, a considerable part of the area would be reserved for cricket-fields, lawn-tennis courts, and other playgrounds, and the clubs using public grounds might perhaps be called upon to contribute to the expense of keeping these in order, as is customary elsewhere.

I. Sewage.

All that need be said on this subject has been said in Chap. i., page 25, and Chap. ii., page 32.

K. Interest.

The money to construct the public works with which we have been dealing is supposed to be borrowed at 4½ per cent. The question here arises—a question partly dealt with in Chap. iv.—what is the security for those who lend money on the "B" debentures?

My answer is three-fold.

(1) Those who advance money to effect any improvements on land have a security the safety of which is in reality largely determined by the effectiveness with which the money so advanced is spent; and, applying this truism, I venture to say that, for effectiveness of expenditure, no money which the investing public has been for many years asked to subscribe for improvements of a like nature has an equal security, whether it be measured by miles of road, acres of park, or numbers of school children well provided for.

(2) Those who advance money to effect improvements

on land have a security the safety of which is largely determined by the consideration, aye or no, are other and yet more valuable works to be simultaneously carried out by others at their own expense, which other works are to become a security in respect of the first-mentioned advance; and, applying this second truism, I say that, as the money for effecting the public improvements here described would only be asked for as and when other improvements—factories, houses, shops, etc. (costing far more money than the public works necessary at any given period)—were about to be built or were in process of building, the quality of the security would be a very high one.

(3) It is difficult to name a better security than that offered when money is to be expended in converting an agricultural estate into an urban, and this of the very best known type.

That the scheme is in reality a 3 per cent. security, and would in its later stages become so, I entertain little doubt; but I do not forget that, though its points of novelty are the very elements which really *make* it secure, they may not make it *seem* so, and that those who are merely looking out for an investment may eye it with some distrust because of its novelty. We shall have in the first instance to look to those who will advance money with somewhat mixed motives—public spirit, love of enterprise, and possibly, as to some persons, with a lurking belief that they will be able to dispose of their debentures at a premium, as they probably will. Therefore, I put down 4½ per cent., but if anyone's conscience prick him he may tender at 2 or 2½, or may even advance money without interest.

L. Sinking Fund.

This sinking fund, which provides for the extinction of the debt in thirty years, compares most favourably with that usually provided by local bodies for works of so permanent a character. The Local Government Board frequently allows loans to be created with a sinking fund extending over much longer periods. It is to be remembered also that an additional sinking fund for the landed estate has been already provided (*see* Chapter iv., p. 42).

M. Balance available for Rates levied by Local Bodies within whose jurisdiction the estate is situated.

It will be seen that the whole scheme of Garden City will make extremely few demands upon the resources of outside local authorities. Roads, sewers, schools, parks, libraries, etc., will be provided out of the funds of the new "municipality," and in this way the whole scheme will come to the agriculturists at present on the estate very much like "a rate in aid"; for, as rates are only raised for the purpose of public expenditure, it follows that, there being little or no fresh call upon the rates while the number of ratepayers is greatly increased, the rate per head must fall. I do not, however, forget that there are some functions which such a voluntary organisation as Garden City could not take over, such as the police and the administration of the poor-law. As to the latter, it is believed that the whole scheme will in the long run make such rates unnecessary, as Garden City will provide, at all events from the time when the estate has been fully paid for, pensions for all its needy old citizens. Meantime and from the very outset it is doing its full share of charitable work. It has allotted sites of 30 acres for various institutions, and at a later stage will doubtless be prepared to assume the whole cost of maintaining them.

With regard to police rates, it is not believed that these can be largely increased by the coming into the town of 30,000 citizens, who, for the most part, will be of the law-abiding class; for, there being but one landlord, and this the community, it will not be difficult to prevent the creation of those surroundings which make the intervention of the police so frequently necessary. (*See* Chapter vii.)

I have, I think, now fully established my contention that the rate-rent which would be willingly offered by the tenants of Garden City, in respect of the advantages afforded them, would be amply sufficient, (1) to pay landlord's rent in the form of interest on debentures; (2) to provide a sinking fund for the entire abolition of landlord's rent; and (3) to provide for the municipal needs of the town without recourse to any Act of Parliament for the enforcement of rates—the community depending solely on the very large powers it possesses as a landlord.

N. Revenue-bearing Expenditure.

If the conclusion already arrived at—that the experiment advocated affords an outlet for an extremely effective expenditure of labour and capital—is sound in regard to objects the cost of which is usually defrayed out of rates, that conclusion must, I think, be equally sound in regard to tramways, lighting, water-supply, and the like, which, when carried on by municipalities, are usually made a source of revenue, thus relieving the ratepayer by making his rates lighter.[1] And as I have added nothing to the proposed revenue for any prospective profits on such undertakings, I do not propose to make any estimate of expenditure.

[1] "Birmingham rates are relieved to the extent of £50,000 a year out of profits on gas. The Electrical Committee of Manchester has promised to pay £10,000 this year to the city fund, in relief of rates out of a net profit of over £16,000."—*Daily Chronicle*, 9th June, 1897.

CHAPTER VI.

ADMINISTRATION.

I HAVE in the 4th and 5th chapters dealt with the fund at the disposal of the Board of Management, and have endeavoured to show, and I believe with success, that the rate-rents collected by the trustees in their capacity of landlords of the towns will suffice, (1) to provide interest on the debentures with which the estate is purchased, (2) to provide a sinking fund which will at a comparatively early date leave the community free from the burden of interest on such debentures, and (3) to enable the Board of Management to carry on such undertakings as are elsewhere, for the most part, carried out by means of rates compulsorily levied.

A most important question now arises regarding the extent to which municipal enterprise is to be carried, and how far it is to supersede private enterprise. We have already by implication stated that the experiment advocated does not involve, as has been the case in so many social experiments—the complete municipalisation of industry and the elimination of private enterprise. But what principle is to guide us in determining the line which shall separate municipal from private control and management? Mr. Joseph Chamberlain has said: "The true field for municipal activity is limited to those things which the community can do better than the individual." Precisely, but that is a truism, and does not carry us one whit further, for the very question at issue is as to *what those things are* which the community can do better than the individual; and when we seek for an answer to this question we find two directly conflicting views—the view of the socialist, who says: Every phase of wealth-production and distribution can be best performed by the community; and the view of the individualist, who contends these things are best left to the individual. But probably the true answer is to be found at neither extreme, is only to be gained by experiment, and will differ in different communities and at different periods. With a growing intelligence and honesty in municipal enterprise, with greater freedom from the control of the Central Government, it may be found—especially on municipally-owned land—that the field of municipal activity may grow so as to embrace a very large area, and yet the municipality claim no rigid monopoly and the fullest rights of combination exist.

Bearing this in mind, the municipality of Garden City will, at the outset, exercise great caution, and not attempt too much. The difficulty of raising the necessary funds with which to carry on municipal undertakings would be greatly increased if the Board of Management attempted to do everything; and, in the prospectus to be ultimately issued, a clear statement will be made of what the Corporation undertakes to do with the moneys entrusted to it, and this will at first embrace little more than those things which experience has proved municipalities can perform better than individuals. Tenants, too, will, it is obvious, be far more ready to offer adequate "rate-rents" if they are given distinctly to understand to what purpose those "rate-rents" are to be devoted, and after those things are done, and done well, little difficulty will be placed in the way of further appropriate extensions of the field of municipal enterprise.

Our answer, then, to the question, what field is to be covered by municipal enterprise, is this. Its extent will be measured simply by the willingness of the tenants to pay rate-rents, and will grow in proportion as municipal work is done efficiently and honestly, or decline as it is done dishonestly or inefficiently. If, for example, the tenants find that a very small additional contribution, recently made in the shape of "rate-rent," has enabled the authorities to provide an excellent supply of water for all purposes, and they are convinced that so good a result at so small a cost would not have been achieved through the agency of any private undertaking working for a profit, they will naturally be willing and even anxious that further hopeful-looking experiments in municipal work should be undertaken. The site of Garden City may, in this respect, be compared with Mr. and Mrs. Boffin's famous apartment, which, the reader of Dickens will remember, was furnished at one end to suit the taste of Mrs. Boffin, who was "a dab at fashion," while at the other end it was furnished to conform to the notions of solid comfort which so gratified Mr. Boffin, but with the mutual understanding between the parties that if Mr. B. should get by degrees to be "a high-flyer" at fashion, then Mrs. B.'s carpet would gradually "come for'arder," whilst if Mrs. B. should become "less of a dab at fashion," Mrs. B.'s carpet would "go back'arder." So, in Garden City, if the inhabitants become greater "dabs" at co-operation, the municipality will "come for'arder"; if they become less "dabs" at co-operation, the municipality will "go back'arder"; while the relative number of positions occupied by municipal workers and non-municipal workers at any period will very fairly reflect the skill and integrity of the public administration and the degree of value which is therefore associated with municipal effort.

But the municipality of Garden City, besides setting its face against any attempt to embark upon too large a field of enterprise, will so frame its constitution that the responsibility for each branch of the municipal service will be thrown directly upon the officers of that branch and not be practically lost sight of because loosely thrown upon the larger central body—a plan which makes it difficult for the public to perceive where any leakage or friction may be taking place. The constitution is modelled upon that of a large and well-appointed business, which is divided into various departments, each department being expected to justify its own continued existence—its officers being selected, not so much for their knowledge of the business generally as for their special fitness for the work of their department.

THE BOARD OF MANAGEMENT

consists of—

(1) The Central Council.
(2) The Departments.

THE CENTRAL COUNCIL (*see* Diagram 5).

In this council (or its nominees) are vested the rights and powers of the community as sole landlord of Garden

City. Into its treasury are paid (after provision has been made for landlord's rent and sinking fund) all rate-rents received from its tenants, as well as the profits derived from its various municipal undertakings, and these, we have seen, are amply sufficient to discharge all public burdens without any resort to the expedient of compulsory rates. The powers possessed by the Central Council are, it may be noticed in passing, more ample than those possessed by other municipal bodies, for whilst most of these enjoy only such powers as are expressly conferred on them by Acts of Parliament, the Central Council of Garden City exercises on behalf of the people those wider rights, powers and privileges which are enjoyed by landlords under the common law. The private owner of land can do with his land and with the revenue he derives from it what he pleases so long as he is not a nuisance to his neighbour; while, on the other hand, public bodies which acquire land or obtain power to levy rates by Acts of Parliament, can only use that land or spend those rates for such purposes as are expressly prescribed by those Acts. But Garden City is in a greatly superior position, for, by stepping as a *quasi* public body into the rights of a private landlord, it becomes at once clothed with far larger powers for carrying out the will of the people than are possessed by other local bodies, and thus solves to a large extent the problem of local self-government.

But the Central Council, though possessing these large powers, delegates many of them, for convenience of administration, to its various departments, retaining, however, responsibility for—

(1) The general plan on which the estate is laid out.

(2) The amount of money voted to each of the various spending departments, as schools, roads, parks, etc.

(3) Such measure of oversight and control of the departments as is necessary to preserve a general unity and harmony, but no more.

THE DEPARTMENTS.

These are divided into various groups—for example:

(A) Public Control.
(B) Engineering.
(C) Social Purposes.

GROUP A, PUBLIC CONTROL.

This group may consist of the following sub-groups:

Finance.	Assessment.
Law.	Inspection.

Finance.

Into this department are paid, after making provision for landlord's rent and sinking fund, all rate-rents; and out of it the necessary sums for the various departments are voted by the Central Council.

Assessment.

This department receives all applications from would-be tenants, and fixes the rate-rent to be paid—such rate-rents not, however, being fixed arbitrarily by the department, but upon the essential principle adopted by other Assessment Committees—the really determining factor being the rate-rent which an average tenant is found willing to pay.[1]

Law.

This department settles the terms and conditions under which leases shall be granted, and the nature of the covenants to be entered into by and with the Central Council.

Inspection.

This department carries out such reasonable duties in relation to inspection as the municipality, in its capacity of landlord, may with the tenants of the municipality mutually agree upon.

GROUP B, ENGINEERING.

This group may consist of the following departments —some of which would be later creations.

Roads.	Parks and open spaces.
Subways.	Drainage.
Sewers.	Canals.
Tramways.	Irrigation.
Municipal Railway.	Water-supply.
Public Buildings (other than schools).	Motive-power & Lighting.
	Messages.

GROUP C, SOCIAL AND EDUCATIONAL.

This group is also divided into various departments, dealing with:—

Education. Libraries.
Baths and Wash-houses.
Music. Recreation.

[1] This individual is known to Assessment Committees under the name of the "hypothetical tenant."

Election of Members of Board of Management.

Members (who may be men or women) are elected by the rate-renters to serve on one or more departments, and the Chairmen and Vice-Chairmen of the departments constitute the Central Council.

Under such a constitution it is believed that the community would have the readiest means of rightly estimating the work of its servants, and, at election times, would have clear and distinct issues brought before it. The candidates would not be expected to specify their views upon a hundred and one questions of municipal policy upon which they had no definite opinions, and which would probably not give rise within their term of office to the necessity for recording their votes, but would simply state their views as to some special question or group of questions, a sound opinion upon which would be of urgent importance to the electors, because immediately connected with the welfare of the town.

CHAPTER VII.

SEMI-MUNICIPAL ENTERPRISE—LOCAL OPTION—TEMPERANCE REFORM.

In the last chapter we saw that no line could be sharply drawn between municipal and individual enterprise, so that one could definitely say of one or the other, "Hitherto shalt thou come, but no further"; and this ever-changing character of the problem can be usefully illustrated in our examination of the industrial life of Garden City by reference to a form of enterprise there carried on which is neither distinctly municipal nor distinctly individualistic, but partaking, as it does, of the character of both, may be termed "semi-municipal."

Among the most reliable sources of revenue possessed by many of our existing municipalities are their so-called "public markets." But it is important to notice that these markets are by no means public in the same full sense as are our public parks, libraries, water undertakings, or those numerous other branches of municipal work which are carried on upon public property, by public officials, at the public expense, and solely with a view to the public advantage. On the contrary, our so-called "public markets" are, for the most part, carried on by private individuals, who pay tolls for the parts of the buildings which they occupy, but who are not, except on a few points, controlled by the municipality, and whose profits are personally enjoyed by the various dealers. Markets may, therefore, be fitly termed *semi-municipal* enterprises.

It would, however, have been scarcely necessary to touch on this question, but that it naturally leads up to the consideration of a form of semi-municipal enterprise which is one of the characteristic features of Garden City. This is to be found in the Crystal Palace, which, it will be remembered, is a wide arcade, skirting the Central Park, in which the most attractive wares on sale in Garden City are exhibited, and, this being a winter garden as well as the great shopping centre, is one of the most favourite resorts of the townspeople. The business at the shops is carried on, not by the municipality, but by various individuals and societies, the number of traders being, however, limited by the principle of local option.

The considerations which have led to this system arise out of the distinction between the cases on the one hand of the manufacturers, and on the other of the distributive societies and shopkeepers who are invited to the town. Thus, for example:—In the case of the manufacturer, say, of boots, though he may be glad of the custom of the people of the town, he is by no means dependent on it; his products go all over the world; and he would scarcely wish that the number of boot manufacturers within the area should be specially limited. He would, in fact, lose more than he would gain by restrictions of this kind. A manufacturer frequently prefers to have others carrying on the same trade in his vicinity; for this gives him a larger choice of skilled workmen or workwomen, who themselves desire it also, because it gives them a larger range of employers.

But in the case of shops and stores the case is entirely different. An individual or a society proposing to open in Garden City, say a drapery store, would be most anxious to know what, if any, arrangements were to be made for limiting the number of his competitors, for he would depend almost entirely on the trade of the town or neighbourhood. Indeed it frequently happens that a private landlord, when laying out a building estate, makes arrangements with his shopkeeping tenants designed to prevent them from being swamped by others in the same trade starting on his estate.

The problem, therefore, seems to be how to make such suitable arrangements as will at once—

(1) Induce tenants of the shopkeeping class to come and start in business, offering to the community adequate rate-rents.

(2) Prevent the absurd and wasteful multiplication of shops referred to in the note at the foot of page 81.

(3) Secure the advantages usually gained (or supposed to be) by competition—such as low prices, wide range of choice, fair dealing, civility, etc.

(4) Avoid the evils attending monopoly.

All these results may be secured by a simple expedient, which will have the effect of converting competition from an active into a latent force to be brought into play or held in reserve. It is, as we have said, an application of the principle of local option. To explain:

—Garden City is the sole landlord, and it can grant to a proposed tenant—we will suppose a co-operative society or an individual trader in drapery or fancy goods—a long lease of a certain amount of space in the Grand Arcade (Crystal Palace), at a certain annual rate-rent; and it can say, in effect, to its tenant, "That site is the only space in that ward which we for the present intend to let to any tenant engaged in your trade. The Arcade is, however, designed to be not only the great shopping centre of the town and district, and the permanent exhibition in which the manufacturers of the town display their wares, but a summer and winter garden. The space this Arcade covers will, therefore, be considerably greater than is actually required for the purposes of shops or stores, if these are kept within reasonable limits. Now, so long as you give satisfaction to the people of the town, none of the space devoted to these recreative purposes will be let to anyone engaged in your calling. It is necessary, however, to guard against monopoly. If, therefore, the people become dissatisfied with your methods of trading, and desire that the force of competition shall be actively brought into play against you, then, on the requisition of a certain number, the necessary space in the Arcade will be allotted by the municipality to some one desirous of starting an opposition store."

Under this arrangement it will be seen the trader will depend upon the good-will of his customers. If he charges prices which are too high; if he misrepresents the quality of his goods; if he does not treat his employees with proper consideration in regard to hours of labour, wages, or other matters, he will run a great risk of losing the good-will of his customers, and the people of the town will have a method of expressing their sentiments regarding him which will be extremely powerful; they will simply invite a new competitor to enter the field. But, on the other hand, as long as he perform his functions wisely and well, his good-will resting on the solid basis of the good-will of his customers, he will be protected. His advantages are, therefore, enormous. In other towns a competitor might enter the field against him at any moment without warning, perhaps at the very time when he had purchased some expensive goods, which, unless sold during the season, could only be realised at an enormous sacrifice. In Garden City, on the other hand, he has full notice of his danger—time to prepare for it and even to avert it. Besides, the members of the community, except for the purpose of bringing a trader to reason, will not only have no interest in bringing a competitor into the field, but their interests will be best served by keeping competition in the background as long as possible. If the fire of competition is brought to bear upon a trader, they must suffer with him. They will lose space they would far rather see devoted to some other purpose—they will be bound to pay higher prices than those at which the first trader could supply them if he would, and they will have to render municipal services to two traders instead of to one, while the two competitors could not afford to pay so large a sum in rate-rent as could the original trader. For in many cases the effect of competition is to make a rise in price absolutely necessary. Thus, A. has a trade of 100 gallons of milk a day, and can, we will suppose, pay his expenses, earn a bare living, and supply his customers with milk, say, at 4d. a quart. But if a competitor enters the field, then A. can only sell *milk and water* at 4d. a quart if he is to continue to pay his way. Thus the competition of shopkeepers absolutely tends not only to ruin the competitors, but to maintain and even to raise prices, and so to lower real wages.[1]

Under this system of local option it will be seen that the tradesmen of the town—be they co-operative societies or individuals—would become, if not strictly or technically so, yet in a very real sense, municipal servants. But they would not be bound up in the red-tape of officialism, and would have the fullest rights and powers of initiation. It would not be by any literal conformity to cast-iron and inflexible rules, but by their skill and judgment in forecasting the wishes and in anticipating the tastes of their constituents, as well as by their integrity and courtesy as business men and women, that they would win and maintain their good-will. They would run certain risks, as all tradesmen must, and in return they would be paid, not of course in the form of salary, but in profits. But the risks they would run would be far less than they must be where competition is unchecked and uncontrolled, while their annual profits in propor-

[1] "It has been calculated by Mr. Neale" ("Economics of Co-operation") "that there are 41,735 separate establishments for 22 of the principal retail trades in London. If for each of these trades there were 648 shops—that is 9 to the square mile, no one would have to go more than a quarter of a mile to the nearest shop. There would be 14,256 shops in all. Assuming that this supply would be sufficient, there are in London 251 shops for every hundred that are really wanted. The general prosperity of the country will be much increased when the capital and labour that are now wastefully employed in the retail trade are set free for other work."—"Economics of Industry," A. and M. P. Marshall, Chap. ix., sec. 10.

tion to capital invested might also be greater. They might even sell considerably below the ordinary rate prevailing elsewhere, but yet, having an assured trade and being able very accurately to gauge demand, they might turn their money over with remarkable frequency. Their working expenses, too, would be absurdly small. They would not have to advertise for customers, though they would doubtless make announcements to them of any novelties; but all that waste of effort and of money which is so frequently expended by tradesmen in order to secure customers or to prevent their going elsewhere, would be quite unnecessary.

And not only would each trader be in a sense a municipal servant, but those in his employ would be also. It is true such a trader would have the fullest right to engage and dismiss his servants; but if he acted arbitrarily or harshly, if he paid insufficient wages, or treated his employees inconsiderately, he would certainly run the risk of losing the good-will of the majority of his customers, even although in other respects he might prove himself an admirable public servant. On the other hand, if the example were set of profit-sharing, this might grow into a custom, and the distinction between master and servant would be gradually lost in the simple process of all becoming co-operators.[1]

This system of local option as applied to shopkeeping is not only business-like, but it affords an opportunity for

[1] This principle of local option, which is chiefly applicable to distributive callings, is perhaps applicable to production in some of its branches. Thus bakeries and laundries, which would largely depend upon the trade of the locality, seem to present instances where it might with some caution be applied. Few businesses seem to require more thorough supervision and

the expression of that public conscience against the sweater which is now being stirred, but which scarcely knows how to effectually respond to the new impulse. Thus there was established in London some years ago the Consumers' League, the object of which was not, as its name might lead one to suspect, to protect the consuming public against the unscrupulous producer, but it was to protect the sweated, over-driven producer against a consuming public over-clamorous for cheapness. Its aim was to assist such of the public as hate and detest the sweating system to avail themselves of the League's carefully compiled information, so that they might be able to studiously avoid the products which had passed through sweaters' hands. But such a movement as the Consumers' League advocated could make but little headway without the support of the shopkeeper. That consumer must be an uncommonly earnest opponent of sweating who insists upon knowing the source whence every article he purchases has come, and a shopkeeper under ordinary circumstances would scarcely be disposed either to give such information or to guarantee that the goods he sold were produced under "fair" conditions; while to establish shops in large cities, which are already overcrowded with distributive agencies, and to do this with the special object of putting down sweating, is to court failure. Here in Garden City, however, there will be a splendid opportunity for the public conscience to express itself in

control than these, and few have a more direct relation to health. Indeed, a very strong case might be made out for municipal bakeries and municipal laundries, and it is evident that the control of an industry by the community is a half-way house to its assumption of it, should this prove desirable and practicable.

this regard, and no shopkeeper will, I hope, venture to sell "sweated goods."

There is another question with which the term "local option" is most closely associated which may be dealt with here. I refer to the temperance question. Now it will be noticed that the municipality, in its position of sole landlord, has the *power* of dealing in the most drastic manner possible with the liquor traffic. There are, as is well known, many landlords who will not permit a public-house to be opened on their estate, and the landlord of Garden City—the people themselves—*could* adopt this course. But would this be wise? I think not. First, such a restriction would keep away the very large and increasing class of moderate drinkers, and would also keep away many of those who are scarcely moderate in their use of alcohol, but as to whom reformers would be most anxious that they should be brought under the healthful influences which would surround them in Garden City. The public-house, or its equivalent, would, in such a community, have many competitors for the favour of the people; while, in large cities, with few opportunities of cheap and rational enjoyment, it has its own way. The experiment, as one in the direction of temperance reform, would, therefore, be more valuable if the traffic were permitted under reasonable regulations than if it were stopped; because, while, in the former case, the effects in the direction of temperance would be clearly traceable to the more natural and healthy form of life, if the latter course were adopted it could only prove, what no one now denies, that it may be possible, by restrictive measures, to entirely keep away the traffic from one small area while intensifying the evils elsewhere.

But the community would certainly take care to prevent the undue multiplication of licensed houses, and it would be free to adopt any one of the various methods which the more moderate of temperance reformers suggest. The municipal authorities might conduct the liquor traffic themselves, and employ the profits in relief of rates. There is, however, much force in the objection that it is not desirable that the revenue of a community should be so derived, and, therefore, it might be better that the profits should be entirely applied to purposes which would compete with the traffic, or in minimising its evil effects by establishing asylums for those affected with alcoholism.[1] On this subject, as on all points involved, I earnestly invite correspondence from those who have practical suggestions to offer; and, although the town is but a small one, it would perhaps not be impracticable to test various promising suggestions in the different wards.

[1] Since "To-Morrow" was published, various Companies have been formed by the Public House Trust Association, 116 Victoria Street, Westminster, S.W., with the object of carrying on the trade on principles advocated by the Bishop of Chester. A limited dividend of 5 per cent. is fixed; all profits beyond are expended in useful public enterprises, and the Managers have no interest whatever in pushing the trade in intoxicating liquors. It may be interesting also to observe that Mr. George Cadbury, in the Deed of Foundation of the Bourneville Trust, provides for the complete restriction of the traffic at the outset. But as a practical man, he sees that as the Trust grows (and its power of growth is among its most admirable features) it may be necessary to remove such complete restrictions. And he provides that in that event "all the net profits arising from the sale and co-operative distribution of intoxicating liquors shall be devoted to securing recreation and counter attractions to the liquor trade as ordinarily conducted."

CHAPTER VIII.

PRO-MUNICIPAL WORK.

There will be found in every progressive community societies and organisations which represent a far higher level of public spirit and enterprise than that possessed or displayed by such communities in their collective capacity. It is probable that the government of a community can never reach a higher tone or work on a higher plane than the average sense of that community demands and enforces; and it will greatly conduce to the well-being of any society if the efforts of its State or municipal organisations are inspired and quickened by those of its members whose ideals of society duty rise higher than the average.[1]

And so it may be in Garden City. There will be discovered many opportunities for public service which

[1] "Only a proportion of each in one society can have nerve enough to grasp the banner of a new truth, and endurance enough to bear it along rugged and untrodden ways. . . . To insist on a whole community being made at once to submit to the reign of new practices and new ideas which have just begun to commend themselves to the most advanced speculative intelligence of the time—this, even if it were a possible process, would do much to make life impracticable and to hurry on social dissolution. . . . A new social state can never establish its ideas unless the persons who hold them confess them openly and give them an honest and effective adherence."—Mr. John Morley, "On Compromise," Chap. v.

neither the community as a whole, nor even a majority of its members, will at first recognise the importance of, or see their way to embrace, and which public services it would be useless, therefore, to expect the municipality to undertake; but those who have the welfare of society at heart will, in the free air of the city, be always able to experiment on their own responsibility, and thus quicken the public conscience and enlarge the public understanding.

The whole of the experiment which this book describes is indeed of this character. It represents pioneer work, which will be carried out by those who have not a merely pious opinion, but an effective belief in the economic, sanitary, and social advantages of common ownership of land, and who, therefore, are not satisfied merely to advocate that those advantages should be secured on the largest scale at the national expense, but are impelled to give their views shape and form as soon as they can see their way to join with a sufficient number of kindred spirits. And what the whole experiment is to the nation, so may what we term "pro-municipal" undertakings be to the community of Garden City or to society generally. Just as the larger experiment is designed to lead the nation into a juster and better system of land tenure and a better and more common-sense view of how towns should be built, so are the various pro-municipal undertakings of Garden City devised by those who are prepared to lead the way in enterprises designed to further the well-being of the town, but who have not as yet succeeded in getting their plans or schemes adopted by the Central Council.

Philanthropic and charitable institutions, religious

societies, and educational agencies of various kinds occupy a very large part in this group of pro-municipal or pro-national agencies, and these have been already referred to, and their nature and purposes are well known. But institutions which aim at the more strictly material side of well-being, such as banks and building societies, may be found here too. Just as the founders of the Penny Bank paved the way for the Post Office Savings Bank, so may some of those who study carefully the experiment of building up Garden City see how useful a bank might be, which, like the Penny Bank, aims not so much at gain for its founders as at the well-being of the community at large. Such a bank might arrange to pay the whole of its net profits or all its profits over a certain fixed rate, into the municipal exchequer, and give to the authorities of the town the option of taking it over should they be convinced of its utility and its general soundness.

There is another large field for pro-municipal activity in the work of building homes for the people. The municipality would be attempting too much if it essayed this task, at least at the outset. To do so would be perhaps to depart too widely from the path which experience has justified, however much might be said in favour of such a course on the part of a municipal body in command of ample funds. The municipality has, however, done much to make the building of bright and beautiful homes for the people possible. It has effectually provided against any overcrowding within its area, thus solving a problem found insoluble in existing cities, and it offers sites of ample size at an average rate of £6 per annum for ground-rent and rates. Having done so much, the municipality will pay heed to the warning of an experienced municipal reformer, whose desire for the extension of municipal enterprise cannot be doubted (Mr. John Burns, M.P., L.C.C.), who has said: "A lot of work has been thrown upon the Works Committee of the London County Council by councillors who are so anxious for its success that they would choke it by a burden of work."

There are, however, other sources to which the workers may look for means to build their own homes. They may form building societies or induce co-operative societies, friendly societies, and trade unions to lend them the necessary money, and to help them to organise the requisite machinery. Granted the existence of the true social spirit, and not its mere letter and name, and that spirit will manifest itself in an infinite variety of ways. There are in this country—who can doubt it?—many individuals and societies who would be ready to raise funds and organise associations for assisting bodies of workmen secure of good wages to build their own homes on favourable terms.

A better security the lenders could scarcely have, especially having regard to the ridiculously small landlord's rent paid by the borrowers. Certain it is that if the building of the homes for these workmen is left to speculative builders of a strongly-pronounced individualistic type, and these reap golden harvests, it will be the fault, amongst others, of those large organisations of working-men which now place their capital in banks, whence it is withdrawn by those who with it "exploit" the very men who have placed it there. It is idle for working-men to complain of this self-imposed exploitation, and to talk of nationalising the entire land and capital of this country under an executive of their own class, until they have first been through an apprenticeship at the humbler task of organising men and women with their own capital in constructive work of a less ambitious character—until they have assisted far more largely than they have yet done in building up capital, not to be wasted in strikes, or employed by capitalists in fighting strikers, but in securing homes and employment for themselves and others on just and honourable terms. The true remedy for capitalist oppression where it exists, is not the strike of *no work*, but the strike of *true work*, and against this last blow the oppressor has no weapon. If labour leaders spent half the energy in co-operative organisation that they now waste in co-operative disorganisation, the end of our present unjust system would be at hand. In Garden City such leaders will have a fair field for the exercise of pro-municipal functions—functions which are exercised for the municipality, though not by it—and the formation of building societies of this type would be of the greatest possible utility.

But would not the amount of capital required for the building of the dwelling-houses of a town of 30,000 be enormous? Some persons with whom I have discussed the question look at the matter thus. So many houses in Garden City at so many hundred of pounds a-piece, capital required so much.[1] This is, of course, quite a mistaken way of regarding the problem. Let us test the matter thus. How many houses have been built in London within the last ten years? Shall we say, at the very roughest of guesses 150,000, costing on an average

[1] The position was so stated by Mr. Buckingham in "National Evils and Practical Remedies," see Chap. x.

£300 a-piece—to say nothing of shops, factories, and warehouses. Well, that is £45,000,000. Was £45,000,000 raised for this purpose? Yes, certainly, or the houses would not have been built. But the money was not raised all at once, and if one could recognise the actual sovereigns that were raised for the building of these 150,000 houses, one would often find the very same coins turning up again and again. So in Garden City. Before it is completed, there will be 5,500 houses at, say, £300 a-piece, making £1,650,000. But this capital will not be raised all at once, and here, far more than in London, the very same sovereigns would be employed in building many houses. For observe, money is not lost or consumed when it is spent. It merely changes hands. A workman of Garden City borrows £200 from a pro-municipal building society, and builds a house with it. That house costs him £200, and the 200 sovereigns disappear so far as he is concerned, but they become the property of the brickmakers, builders, carpenters, plumbers, plasterers, etc., who have built his house, whence those sovereigns would find their way into the pockets of the tradesmen and others with whom such workmen deal, and thence would pass into the pro-municipal bank of the town, when presently, those 200 identical sovereigns might be drawn out and employed in building another house. Thus there would be presented the apparent anomaly of two, and then three, and then four or more houses, each costing £200, being built with 200 sovereigns.[1] But there is no real anomaly about it. The coins, of course,

[1] A similar line of argument to this is very fully elaborated in a most able work entitled "The Physiology of Industry," by Mummery and Hobson (MacMillan & Co.).

did not build the houses in any of the supposed cases. The coins were but the measure of value, and like a pair of scales and weights, may be used over and over again without any perceptible lessening of their worth. What built the houses was really labour, skill, enterprise, working up the free gifts of nature; and though each of the workers might have his reward weighed out to him in coins, the cost of all buildings and works in Garden City must be mainly determined by the skill and energy with which its labours are directed. Still, so long as gold and silver are recognised as the medium of exchange, it will be necessary to use them, and of great importance to use them skilfully—for the skill with which they are used, or their unnecessary use dispensed with, as in a banker's clearing house, will have a most important bearing upon the cost of the town, and upon the annual tax levied in the shape of interest on borrowed capital. Skill must be therefore directed to the object of so using coins that they may quickly effect their object of measuring one value, and be set to work to measure another—that they may be turned over as many times as possible in the year, in order that the amount of labour measured by each coin may be as large as possible, and thus the amount represented by interest on the coins borrowed, though paid at the normal or usual rate, shall bear as small a proportion as possible to the amount paid to labour. If this is done effectively, then a saving to the community in respect of interest as great as the more easily demonstrated saving in landlord's rent may probably be effected.

And now the reader is asked to observe how admirably, and, as it were, automatically, a well-organised migratory movement to land held in common lends itself to the economic use of money, and to the making of one coin serve many purposes. Money, it is often said, is "a drug in the market." Like labour itself, it seems enchanted, and thus one sees millions in gold and silver lying idle in banks facing the very streets where men are wandering workless and penniless. But here, on the site of Garden City, the cry for employment on the part of those willing to work will no more be heard in vain. Only yesterday it may have been so, but to-day the enchanted land is awake, and is loudly calling for its children. There is no difficulty in finding work—profitable work—work that is really urgently, imperatively needed—the building of a home-city, and, as men hasten to build up this and the other towns which must inevitably follow its construction, the migration to the towns—the old, crowded, chaotic slum-towns of the past—will be effectually checked, and the current of population set in precisely the opposite direction—to the new towns, bright and fair, wholesome and beautiful.

CHAPTER IX.

SOME DIFFICULTIES CONSIDERED.

HAVING now, in a concrete rather than an abstract form, stated the objects and purposes of our scheme, it may be well to deal, though somewhat briefly, with an objection which may arise in the thought of the reader: "Your scheme may be very attractive, but it is but one of a great number, many of which have been tried and have met with but little success. How do you distinguish it from those? How, in the face of such a record of failure, do you expect to secure that large measure of public support which is necessary ere such a scheme can be put into operation?"

The question is a very natural one, and demands an answer. My reply is: It is quite true that the pathway of experiment towards a better state of society is strewn with failures. But so is the pathway of experiment to any result that is worth achieving. Success is, for the most part, built on failure. As Mrs. Humphrey Ward remarks in "Robert Elsmere": "All great changes are preceded by numbers of sporadic, and, as the bystander thinks, intermittent efforts." A successful invention or discovery is usually a slow growth, to which new elements are added, and from which old elements are removed, first in the thought of the inventor, and subsequently in an outward form, until at last precisely the right elements and no others are brought together. Indeed, it may be truly said that if you find a series of experiments continued through many years by various workers, there will eventually be produced the result for which so many have been industriously searching. Long-continued effort, in spite of failure and defeat, is the fore-runner of complete success. He who wishes to achieve success may turn past defeat into future victory by observing one condition. He must profit by past experiences, and aim at retaining all the strong points without the weaknesses of former efforts.

To deal at all exhaustively here with the history of social experiments would be beyond the scope of this book; but a few leading features may be noticed with a view of meeting the objection with which this chapter opens.

Probably the chief cause of failure in former social experiments has been a misconception of the principal element in the problem—human nature itself. The degree of strain which average human nature will bear in an altruistic direction has not been duly considered by those who have essayed the task of suggesting new forms of social organisation. A kindred mistake has arisen from regarding one principle of action to the exclusion of others. Take Communism, for instance. Communism is a most excellent principle, and all of us are Communists in some degree, even those who would shudder at being told so. For we all believe in communistic roads, communistic parks, and communistic libraries. But though Communism is an excellent principle, Individualism is no less excellent. A great orchestra which enraptures us with its delightful music is composed of men and women who are accustomed not only to play together, but to practise separately, and to delight themselves and their friends by their own, it may be comparatively, feeble efforts. Nay, more: isolated and individual thought and action are as essential, if the best results of combination are to be secured, as combination and co-operation are essential, if the best results of isolated effort are to be gained. It is by isolated thought that new combinations are worked out; it is through the lessons learned in associated effort that the best individual work is accomplished; and that society will prove the most healthy and vigorous where the freest and fullest opportunities are afforded alike for individual and for combined effort.

Now, do not the whole series of communistic experiments owe their failure largely to this—that they have not recognised this duality of principle, but have carried one principle, excellent enough in itself, altogether too far? They have assumed that because common property is good, all property should be common; that because associated effort can produce marvels, individual effort is to be regarded as dangerous, or at least futile, some extremists even seeking to abolish altogether the idea of the family or home. No reader will confuse the experiment here advocated with any experiment in absolute Communism.

Nor is the scheme to be regarded as a socialistic experiment. Socialists, who may be regarded as Communists of a more moderate type, advocate common property in land and in all the instruments of production, distribution, and exchange—railways, machinery, factories, docks, banks, and the like; but they would preserve the principle of private ownership in all such things as have passed in the form of wages to the servants of the community, with the proviso, however, that these wages shall not be employed in organised creative effort, involving the employment of more than one person; for all forms of employment with a view to remuneration should, as the Socialists contend, be under the direction of some recognised department of the Government, which is to claim a rigid monopoly. But it is very doubtful whether this principle of the Socialist, in which there is a certain measure of recognition of the individual side of man's nature as well as of his social side, represents a basis on which an experiment can fairly proceed with the hope of permanent success. Two chief difficulties appear to present themselves. First, the self-seeking side of man—his too frequent desire to produce, with a view to possessing for his own personal use and enjoyment; and, secondly, his love of independence and of initiative, his personal ambition, and his consequent unwillingness to put himself under the guidance of others for the whole of his working day, with little opportunity of striking out some independent line of action, or of taking a leading part in the creation of new forms of enterprise.

Now, even if we pass over the first difficulty—that of human self-seeking—even if we assume that we have a body of men and women who have realised the truth that concerted social effort will achieve far better results in enjoyable commodities for each member of the community than can possibly be achieved by ordinary competitive methods—each struggling for himself—we have still the other difficulty, arising out of the higher and not the lower nature of the men and women who are to be organised—their love of independence and of initiative. Men love combined effort, but they love individual effort, too, and they will not be content with such few opportunities for personal effort as they would be allowed to make in a rigid socialistic community. Men do not object to being organised under competent leadership, but some also want to be leaders, and to have a share in the work of organising; they like to lead as well as to be led. Besides, one can easily imagine men filled with a desire to serve the community in some way which the community as a whole did not at the moment appreciate the advantage of, and who would be precluded by the very constitution of the socialistic state from carrying their proposals into effect.

Now, it is at this very point that a most interesting experiment at Topolobampo has broken down. The experiment, which was initiated by Mr. A. K. Owen, an American civil engineer, was started on a considerable tract of land obtained under concession from the Mexican Government. One principle adopted by Mr. Owen was that "all employment must be through the Department for the Diversity of Home Industries. One member cannot directly employ another member, and only members can be employed through the settlement."[1] In other words, if A. and B. were dissatisfied with the management, whether owing to doubts as to its competency or honesty, they could not arrange to work with each other, even though their sole desire might be the common good; but they must leave the settlement. And

[1] "Integral Co-operation at Work," A. K. Owen (U.S. Book Co., 150 Worth St., N.Y.).

this is what they accordingly did in very considerable numbers.

It is at this point that a great distinction between the Topolobampo experiment and the scheme advocated in this work is evident. In Topolobampo the organisation claimed a monopoly of all productive work, and each member must work under the direction of those who controlled that monopoly, or must leave the organisation. In Garden City no such monopoly is claimed, and any dissatisfaction with the public administration of the affairs of the town would no more necessarily lead to a widespread split in Garden City than in any other municipality. At the outset, at least, by far the larger part of the work done will be by individuals or combinations of individuals quite other than municipal servants, just as in any other municipality, at present existing, the sphere of municipal work is still very small as compared with the work performed by other groups.

Other sources of failure in some social experiments are the considerable expense incurred by migrants before they reach the scene of their future labours, the great distance from any large market, and the difficulty of previously obtaining any real knowledge of the conditions of life and labour there prevailing. The one advantage gained—cheap land—seems to be altogether insufficient to compensate for these and other disadvantages.

We now come to what is perhaps the chief difference between the scheme advocated in this work and most other schemes of a like nature which have been hitherto advocated or put into actual practice. That difference is this: While others have sought to weld into one large organisation individuals who have not yet been combined into smaller groups, or who must leave those smaller groups on their joining the larger organisation, my proposal appeals not only to individuals but to co-operators, manufacturers, philanthropic societies, and others experienced in organisation, and with organisations under their control, to come and place themselves under conditions involving no new restraints but rather securing wider freedom. And, further, a striking feature of the present scheme is that the very considerable number of persons already engaged on the estate will not be displaced (except those on the town site, and these gradually), but these will themselves form a valuable nucleus, paying in rents, from the very inception of the enterprise, a sum which will go very far towards the interest on the money with which the estate is purchased—rents which they will be more willing to pay to a landlord who will treat them with perfect equity, and who will bring to their doors consumers for their produce. The work of organisation is, therefore, in a very large measure accomplished. The army is now in existence; it has but to be mobilised; it is with no undisciplined mob that we have to deal. Or the comparison between this experiment and those which have preceded it is like that between two machines—one of which has to be created out of various ores which have first to be gathered together and then cast into various shapes, while for the other all the parts are ready to hand and have but to be fitted together.

CHAPTER X.

A UNIQUE COMBINATION OF PROPOSALS.

In the last chapter, I pointed out the great differences of principle between the project placed before the reader of this work and some of those schemes of social reform which, having been put to the test of experience, have ended in disaster, and I urged that there were features of the proposed experiment which so completely distinguished it from those unsuccessful schemes that they could not be fairly regarded as any indication of the results which would probably follow from launching this experiment.

It is my present purpose to show that though the scheme taken as a whole is a new one, and is, perhaps, entitled to some consideration on that account, its chief claim upon the attention of the public lies in the fact that it combines the important features of several schemes which have been advocated at various times, and so combines them as to secure the best results of each, without the dangers and difficulties which sometimes, even in the minds of their authors, were clearly and distinctly seen.

Shortly stated, my scheme is a combination of three distinct projects which have, I think, never been united before. These are—(1) The proposals for an organised migratory movement of population of Wakefield and of Professor Marshall; (2) the system of land tenure first proposed by Thos. Spence and afterwards (though with an important modification) by Mr. Herbert Spencer; and (3) the model city of Jas. S. Buckingham.[1]

Let us take these proposals in the order named. Wakefield, in his "Art of Colonisation" (London: J. W. Parker, 1849), urged that colonies when formed—he was not thinking of home colonies—should be based on scientific principles. He said (page 109): "We send out colonies of the limbs, without the belly and the head, of needy persons, many of them mere paupers, or even criminals; colonies made up of *a single class of persons* in the community, and that the most helpless and the most unfit to perpetuate our national character, and to become the fathers of a race whose habits of thinking and feeling shall correspond to those which, in the meantime, we are cherishing at home. The ancients, on the contrary, sent out *a representation of the parent State—colonists from all ranks.* We stock the farm with creeping and climbing plants, without any trees of firmer growth for them to entwine round. A hop-ground without poles, the plants matted confusedly together, and scrambling on the ground in tangled heaps, with here and

[1] I may, perhaps, state as showing how in the search for truth men's minds run in the same channels, and as, possibly, some additional argument for the soundness of the proposals thus combined, that, till I had got far on with my project, I had not seen either the proposals of Professor Marshall or of Wakefield (beyond a very short reference to the latter in J. S. Mill's "Elements of Political Economy"), nor had I seen the work of Buckingham, which, published nearly fifty years ago, seems to have attracted but little attention.

there some clinging to rank thistles and hemlock, would be an apt emblem of a modern colony. The ancients began by nominating to the honourable office of captain or leader of the colony one of the chief men, if not the chief man of the State, like the queen bee leading the workers. Monarchies provided a prince of the royal blood; an aristocracy its choicest nobleman; a democracy its most influential citizen. These naturally carried along with them some of their own station in life—their companions and friends; some of their immediate dependents also—of those between themselves and the lowest class; and were encouraged in various ways to do so. The lowest class again followed with alacrity, because they found themselves moving *with* and not *away from* the state of society in which they had been living. It was the same social and political union under which they had been born and bred; and to prevent any contrary impression being made, the utmost solemnity was observed in transferring the rites of pagan superstition. They carried with them their gods, their festivals, their games—all, in short, that held together and kept entire the fabric of society as it existed in the parent state. Nothing was left behind that could be moved of all that the heart or eye of an exile misses. The new colony was made to appear as if time or chance had reduced the whole community to smaller dimensions, leaving it still essentially the same home and country to its surviving members. It consisted of a general contribution of members from all classes, and so became, on its first settlement, a mature state, with all the component parts of that which sent it forth. It was a transfer of population, therefore, which gave rise to no sense of degradation, as if the colonist were thrust out from a higher to a lower description of community."

J. S. Mill, in his "Elements of Political Economy," Book I., Chap. viii., § 3, says of this work: "Wakefield's theory of colonisation has excited much attention, and is doubtless destined to excite much more. . . . His system consists of arrangements for securing that each colony shall have from the first a town population bearing due proportion to the agricultural, and that the cultivators of the soil shall not be so widely scattered as to be deprived by distance of the benefit of that town population as a market for their produce."

Professor Marshall's proposals for an organised migratory movement of population from London have been already noticed, but the following passage from the article already referred to may be quoted:—

"There might be great variety of method, but the general plan would probably be for a committee, whether formed specially for the purpose or not, to interest themselves in the formation of a colony in some place well beyond the range of London smoke. After seeing their way to building or buying suitable cottages there, they would enter into communication with some of the employers of low-waged labour. They would select, at first, industries that used very little fixed capital; and, as we have seen, it fortunately happens that most of the industries which it is important to move are of this kind. They would find an employer—and there must be many such—who really cares for the misery of his employees. Acting with him and by his advice, they would make themselves the friends of people employed or fit to be employed in his trade; they would show them the advantages of moving, and help them to move, both with counsel and money. They would organise the sending of work backwards and forwards, the employer perhaps opening an agency in the colony. But after being once started it ought to be self-supporting, for the cost of carriage, even if the employees went in sometimes to get instructions, would be less than the saving made in rent—at all events, if allowance be made for the value of the garden produce. And more than as much gain would probably be saved by removing the temptation to drink which is caused by the sadness of London. They would meet with much passive resistance at first. The unknown has terrors to all, but especially to those who have lost their natural spring. Those who have lived always in the obscurity of a London court might shrink away from the free light; poor as are their acquaintanceships at home, they might fear to go where they knew no one. But, with gentle insistence, the committee would urge their way, trying to get those who knew one another to move together, by warm, patient sympathy, taking off the chill of the first change. It is only the first step that costs; every succeeding step would be easier. The work of several firms, not always in the same business, might, in some cases, be sent together. Gradually a prosperous industrial district would grow up, and then, mere self-interest would induce employers to bring down their main workshops, and even to start factories in the colony. Ultimately all would gain, but most the landowners and the railroads connected with the colony."

What could more strongly point than the last sentence of that quotation from Professor Marshall's proposal to the necessity of first *buying* the land, so that the most admirable project of Thomas Spence can be put into practice, and thus prevent the terrible rise in rent which Professor Marshall forsees? Spence's proposal, put forward more than a hundred years ago, at once suggests how to secure the desired end. Here it is:—

"Then you may behold the rent which the people have paid into the parish treasuries employed by each parish in paying the Government its share of the sum which the Parliament or National Congress at any time grants; in maintaining and relieving its own poor and people out of work; in paying the necessary officers their salaries; in building, repairing, and adorning its houses, bridges, and other structures; in making and maintaining convenient and delightful streets, highways, and passages, both for foot and carriages; in making and maintaining canals and other conveniences for trade and navigation; in planting and taking in waste grounds; in premiums for the encouragement of agriculture or anything else thought worthy of encouragement; and, in a word, in doing whatever the people think proper, and not, as formerly, to support and spread luxury, pride, and all manner of vice. . . . There are no tolls or taxes of any kind paid among them by native or foreigner but the aforesaid rent, which every person pays to the parish, according to the quantity, quality, and conveniences of the land . . . he occupies in it. The government, poor, roads, etc., . . . are all maintained with the rent, on which account all wares, manufactures, allowable trade employments or actions are entirely duty-free."—From a lecture read at the Philosophical Society in Newcastle, on November 8th, 1775, for printing which the Society did the author the honour to expel him.

It will be observed that the only difference between this proposal and the proposals as to land reform put forward in this book, is not a difference of system, but a difference (and a very important one) as to the *method* of its inauguration. Spence appears to have thought that the people would, by a fiat, dispossess the existing owners and establish the system at once and universally throughout the country; while, in this work, it is proposed to purchase the necessary land with which to establish the system on a small scale, and to trust to the inherent advantages of the system leading to its gradual adoption.

Writing some seventy years after Spence had put forward his proposal, Mr. Herbert Spencer (having first laid down the grand principle that all men are equally entitled to the use of the earth, as a corollary of the law of equal liberty generally), in discussing this subject, observes, with his usual force and clearness:—

"But to what does this doctrine that men are equally entitled to the use of the earth, lead? Must we return to the times of unenclosed wilds, and subsist on roots, berries, and game? Or are we to be left to the management of Messrs. Fourrier, Owen, Louis Blanc & Co.? Neither. Such a doctrine is consistent with the highest civilisation, may be carried out without involving a community of goods, and need cause no very serious revolution in existing arrangements. The change required would be simply a change of landlords. Separate ownership would merge in the joint-stock ownership of the public. Instead of being in the possession of individuals, the country would be held by the great corporate body—society. Instead of leasing his acres from an isolated proprietor, the farmer would lease them from the nation. Instead of paying his rent to the agent of Sir John and His Grace, he would pay it to an agent or deputy agent of the community. Stewards would be public officials instead of private ones, and tenancy the only land tenure. A state of things so ordered would be in perfect harmony with the moral law. Under it all men would be equally landlords; all men would be alike free to become tenants. A., B., C. and the rest might compete for a vacant farm as now, and one of them might take that farm without in any way violating the principles of pure equity. All would be equally free to bid; all would be equally free to refrain. And when the farm had been let to A., B., or C., all parties would have done that which they willed, the one in choosing to pay a given sum to his fellow-men for the use of certain lands—the others in refusing to pay the sum. Clearly, therefore, on such a system the earth might be enclosed, occupied, and cultivated in entire subordination to the law of equal freedom."—"Social Statics," Chap. ix., sec. 8.

But having thus written, Mr. Herbert Spencer at a later period, having discovered two grave difficulties in the way of his own proposal, unreservedly withdrew it. The first of these difficulties was the evils which he considered as inseparable from State ownership (see "Justice," published in 1891, appendix B., p. 290); the second, the impossibility, as Mr. Spencer regarded it, of acquiring the land on terms which would be at once equitable to existing owners and remunerative to the community.

But if the reader examines the scheme of Spence, which preceded the now-withdrawn proposals of Mr.

Herbert Spencer, he will see that Spence's scheme was entirely freed (as is the one put forward in this little book), from the objections which might probably attend control by the State.[1] The rents were, under Spence's proposals, as in my own, not to be levied by a *Central Government* far removed from contact with the people, but by the very parish (in my scheme the municipality) in which the people reside. As to the other difficulty which presented itself to Mr. Herbert Spencer's mind—that of acquiring the land on equitable terms, and of yet making it remunerative to the purchasers—a difficulty which Mr. Herbert Spencer, seeing no way out of, rashly concluded to be insuperable—that difficulty is entirely removed by my proposal of buying agricultural or sparsely-settled land, letting it in the manner advocated by Spence, and then bringing about the scientific migratory movement advocated by Wakefield and (though in a somewhat less daring fashion) by Professor Marshall.

Surely a project, which thus brings what Mr. Herbert Spencer still terms "the dictum of absolute ethics"—that all men are equally entitled to the use of the earth—into the field of practical life, and makes it a thing immediately realisable by those who believe in it, must be one of the greatest public importance. When a great philosopher in effect says, we cannot conform our life to the highest moral principles because men have laid an immoral

[1] Though Mr. Herbert Spencer, as if to rebuke his own theory that State control is inherently bad, says, "Political speculation which sets out with the assumption that the State has in all cases the same nature must end in profoundly erroneous conclusions."

foundation for us in the past, but "if, while possessing those ethical sentiments which social discipline has now produced, men stood in possession of a territory not yet individually portioned out, they would no more hesitate to assert equality of their claims to the land than they would hesitate to assert equality of their claims to light and air"[1]—one cannot help wishing—so inharmonious does life seem—that the opportunity presented itself of migrating to a new planet where the "ethical sentiments which social discipline has now produced" might be indulged in. But a new planet, or even "a territory not yet individually portioned out," is by no means necessary if we are but in real earnest; for it has been shown that an organised, migratory movement from over-developed, high-priced land to comparatively raw and unoccupied land, will enable all who desire it to live this life of equal freedom and opportunity; and a sense of the possibility of a life on earth at once orderly and free dawns upon the heart and mind.

The third proposal which I have combined with those of Spence and Mr. Herbert Spencer, of Wakefield and Professor Marshall, embraces one essential feature of a scheme of James S. Buckingham,[2] though I have purposely omitted some of the essential features of that scheme. Mr. Buckingham says (p. 25): "My thoughts were thus directed to the great defects of all existing towns, and the desirability of forming at least one model

[1] "Justice," Chap. xi., p. 85.

[2] Buckingham's scheme is set forth in a work entitled "National Evils and Practical Remedies," published by Peter Jackson, St. Martins le Grand, about 1849.

town which should avoid the most prominent of these defects, and substitute advantages not yet possessed by any." In his work he exhibits a ground plan and a sketch of a town of about 1,000 acres, containing a population of 25,000, and surrounded by a large agricultural estate. Buckingham, like Wakefield, saw the great advantages to be derived by combining an agricultural community with an industrial, and urged: "Wherever practicable, the labours of agriculture and manufacture to be so mingled and the variety of fabrics and materials to be wrought upon also so assorted as to make short periods of labour on each alternately with others produce that satisfaction and freedom from tedium and weariness which an unbroken round of monotonous occupation so frequently occasions, and because also variety of employment develops the mental as well as physical faculties much more perfectly than any single occupation."

But though on these points the scheme is strikingly like my own, it is also a very different one. Buckingham having traced, as he thought, the evils of society to their source in competition, intemperance, and war, proposed to annihilate competition by forming a system of complete or integral co-operation; to remove intemperance by the total exclusion of intoxicants; to put an end to war by the absolute prohibition of gunpowder. He proposed to form a large company, with a capital of £4,000,000; to buy a large estate, and to erect churches, schools, factories, warehouses, dining-halls, dwelling-houses, at rents varying from £30 a year to £300 a year; and to carry on all productive operations, whether agricultural or industrial, as one large undertaking covering the whole field and permitting no rivals.

Now it will be seen that though in outward form Buckingham's scheme and my own present the same feature of a model town set in a large agricultural estate, so that industrial and farming pursuits might be carried on in a healthy, natural way, yet the inner life of the two communities would be entirely different—the inhabitants of Garden City enjoying the fullest rights of free association, and exhibiting the most varied forms of individual and co-operative work and endeavour, the members of Buckingham's city being held together by the bonds of a rigid cast-iron organisation, from which there could be no escape but by leaving the association, or breaking it up into various sections.

To sum up this chapter. My proposal is that there should be an earnest attempt made to organise a migratory movement of population from our overcrowded centres to sparsely-settled rural districts; that the mind of the public should not be confused, or the efforts of organisers wasted in a premature attempt to accomplish this work on a national scale, but that great thought and attention shall be first concentrated on a single movement yet one sufficiently large to be at once attractive and resourceful; that the migrants shall be guaranteed (by the making of suitable arrangements before the movement commences) that the whole increase in land-values due to their migration shall be secured to them; that this be done by creating an organisation, which, while permitting its members to do those things which are good in their own eyes (provided they infringe not the rights of others) shall receive all "rate-rents" and expend them in those public works which the migratory movement renders necessary or expedient—thus eliminating rates, or, at least, greatly reducing the necessity for any compulsory levy; and that the golden opportunity afforded by the fact that the land to be settled upon has but few buildings or works upon it, shall be availed of in the fullest manner, by so laying out a Garden City that, as it grows, the free gifts of Nature—fresh air, sunlight, breathing room and playing room—shall be still retained in all needed abundance, and by so employing the resources of modern science that Art may supplement Nature, and life may become an abiding joy and delight. And it is important to notice that this proposal, so imperfectly put forward, is no scheme hatched in a restless night in the fevered brain of an enthusiast, but is one having its origin in the thoughtful study of many minds, and the patient effort of many earnest souls, each bringing some element of value, till, the time and the opportunity having come, the smallest skill avails to weld those elements into an effective combination.

CHAPTER XI

THE PATH FOLLOWED UP.

"How can a man learn to know himself? By reflection never—only by action. In the measure that thou seekest to do thy duty shalt thou know what is in thee. But what is thy duty? The demand of the hour."—*Goethe*.

THE reader is now asked to kindly assume, for the sake of argument, that our Garden City experiment has been fairly launched, and is a decided success, and to consider briefly some of the more important effects which such an object-lesson, by the light which it will throw upon the pathway of reform, must inevitably produce upon society, and then we will endeavour to trace some of the broader features of the after-development.

Among the greatest needs of man and of society to-day, as at all times, are these: A worthy aim and opportunity to realise it; work and ends worth working for. All that a man is, and all that he may become, is summed up in his aspirations, and this is no less true of society than of the individual. The end I venture to now set before the people of this country and of other countries is no less "noble and adequate" than this, that they should forthwith gird themselves to the task of building up clusters of beautiful home-towns, each zoned by gardens, for those who now dwell in crowded, slum-infested cities. We have already seen how *one* such town may be built; let us now see how the true path of reform, once discovered, will, if resolutely followed, lead society on to a far higher destiny than it has ever yet ventured to hope for, though such a future has often been foretold by daring spirits.

There have in the past been inventions and discoveries on the making of which society has suddenly leaped upward to a new and higher plane of existence. The utilisation of steam—a force long recognised, but which proved somewhat difficult to harness to the task it was fitted to accomplish—effected mighty changes; but the discovery of a method for giving effect to a far greater force than the force of steam—to the long pent-up desire for a better and nobler social life here on earth—will work changes even more remarkable.

What clearly marked economic truth is brought into view by the successful issue of such an experiment as we have been advocating? This:—That there is a broad path open, through a creation of new wealth forms, to a new industrial system in which the productive forces of society and of nature may be used with far greater effectiveness than at present, and in which the distribution of the wealth forms so created will take place on a far juster and more equitable basis. Society may have more to divide among its members, and at the same time the greater dividend may be divided in a juster manner.

Speaking broadly, industrial reformers may be divided into two camps. The first camp includes those who urge the primary importance of paying close and constant attention to the necessity of *increased production:* the second includes those whose special aim is directed to *more just and equitable division.* The former are constantly saying, in effect, "Increase the national dividend, and all will be well"; the latter, "The national dividend is fairly sufficient were it but divided equitably." The former are for the most part of the individualistic, the latter of the socialistic type.

As an instance of the former point of view, I may cite the words of Mr. A. J. Balfour, who, at a Conference of the National Union of Conservative Associations held at Sunderland on 14th November, 1894, said: "Those who represented society as if it consisted of two sections disputing over their share of the general produce were utterly mistaken as to the real bearing of the great social problem. We had to consider that the produce of the country was not a fixed quantity, of which, if the employers got more, the employed would get less, or if the employed got more, the employers would get less. The real question for the working-classes of this country was not primarily or fundamentally a question of division: it was a question of production." As an instance of the second point of view, take the following: "The absurdity of the notion of raising the poor without, to a corresponding degree, depressing the rich will be obvious."—"Principles of Socialism made plain," by Frank Fairman (William Reeves, 83 Charing Cross Road, W.C.), page 33.

I have already shown, and I hope to make this contention yet more clear, that there is a path along which sooner or later, both the Individualist and the Socialist must inevitably travel; for I have made it abundantly clear that on a small scale society may readily become more individualistic than now—if by Individualism is meant a society in which there is fuller and freer opportunity for its members to do and to produce what they will, and to form free associations, of the most varied kinds; while it may also become more socialistic—if by Socialism is meant a condition of life in which the well-being of the community is safe-guarded, and in which the collective spirit is manifested by a wide extension of the area of municipal effort. To achieve these desirable ends, I have taken a leaf out of the books of each type of reformer and bound them together by a thread of practicability. Not content with *urging* the necessity of increased production, I have shown *how it can be achieved;* while the other and equally important end of more equitable distribution is, as I have shown, easily possible, and in a manner which need cause no ill-will, strife, or bitterness; is constitutional; requires no revolutionary legislation; and involves no direct attack upon vested interests. Thus may the desires of the two sections of reformers to whom I have referred be attained. I have, in short, followed out Lord Rosebery's suggestion, and "borrowed from Socialism its large conception of common effort, and its vigorous conception of municipal life, and from Individualism the preservation of self-respect and self-reliance," and, by a concrete illustration, I have, I think, disproved the cardinal contention of Mr. Benjamin Kidd in his famous book, "Social Evolution," that "the interests of the social organism and of the individuals comprising it at any particular time are actually antagonistic; they can never be reconciled; they are inherently and essentially irreconcilable" (page 85).

Most socialistic writers appear to me to exhibit too keen a desire to appropriate old forms of wealth, either by purchasing out or by taxing out the owners, and they seem to have little conception that the truer method is to create new forms and to create them under juster conditions. But this latter conception should inevitably follow an adequate realisation of the ephemeral nature of most forms of wealth; and there is no truth more fully recognised by economic writers than that nearly all forms of material wealth, except, indeed, the planet on which we live and the elements of nature, are extremely fugitive and prone to decay. Thus for instance, J. S. Mill, in "Elements of Political Economy," Book 1, Chapter v., says: "The greater part in value of the wealth now existing in England has been produced by human hands within the last twelve months. A very small proportion indeed of that large aggregate was in existence ten years ago;—of the present productive capital of the country, scarcely any part except farm-houses and manufactories and a few ships and machines; and even these would not in most cases have survived so long if fresh labour had not been employed within that period in putting them into repair. The land subsists, and the land is almost the only thing that subsists." The leaders of the great socialistic movement, of course, know all this perfectly well; yet this quite elementary truth seems to fade from their minds when they are discussing methods of reform, and they appear to be as anxious to seize upon present forms of wealth as if they regarded them as of a really lasting and permanent nature.

But this inconsistency of socialistic writers is all the more striking when one remembers that these writers are the very ones who insist most strongly upon the view that a very large part of the wealth-forms now in existence are not really *wealth* at all—that they are "ilth," and that any form of society which represents even a step towards their ideal must involve the sweeping away of such forms and the creation of new forms in their place. With a degree of inconsistency that is positively startling, they exhibit an insatiable desire to become possessed of these forms of wealth which are not only rapidly decaying, but are in their opinion absolutely useless or injurious.

Thus Mr Hyndman, at a lecture delivered at the Democratic Club, 29th March, 1893, said:—"It was desirable that they should map out and formulate socialistic ideas which they should desire to see brought about when the so-called Individualism of the present day has broken down, as it inevitably would do. One of the first things that they as Socialists would have to do would be to depopulate the vast centres of their overcrowded cities. Their large towns had no longer any large agricultural population from which to recruit their ranks, and through bad and insufficient food, vitiated atmosphere, and other insanitary conditions, the physique of the masses of the cities was rapidly deteriorating, both materially and physically." Precisely; but does not Mr. Hyndman see that in striving to become possessed of present wealth forms, he is laying siege to the wrong fortress? If the population of London, or a large part of the population of London, is to be transplanted elsewhere, when some future event has happened, would it not be well to see if we cannot induce large numbers of these people to transplant themselves *now*, when the problem of London administration and of London reform would, as we shall shortly discover, present itself in a somewhat startling fashion?

A similar inconsistency is to be noticed in a little

book which has had an enormous and well-deserved sale, "Merrie England" (Clarion Offices, Fleet Street). The author, "Nunquam," remarks at the outset: "The problem we have to consider is:—Given a country and a people, find how the people may make the best of the country and themselves." He then proceeds to vigorously condemn our cities, with their houses ugly and mean, their narrow streets, their want of gardens, and emphasises the advantages of out-door occupations. He condemns the factory system, and says: "I would set men to grow wheat and fruit, and rear cattle and poultry for our own use. Then I would develop the fisheries, and construct great fish-breeding lakes and harbours. Then I would restrict our mines, furnaces, chemical works, and factories to the number actually needed for the supply of our own people. Then I would stop the smoke nuisance by developing water-power and electricity. *In order to achieve these ends, I would make all the lands, mills, mines, factories, works, shops, ships, and railways the property of the people.*" That is (the italics are my own), the people are to struggle hard to become possessed of factories, mills, works, and shops, at least half of which must be closed if Nunquam's desires are attained; of ships which will become useless if our foreign trade is to be abandoned, (*see* "Merrie England," Chap. iv.); and of railways, which, with an entire redistribution of population such as Nunquam desires, must for the most part become derelict. And how long is this useless struggle to last? Would it not—I ask Nunquam to consider this point carefully—be better to study a smaller problem first, and, to paraphrase his words, "Given, say, 6,000 acres of land, let us endeavour to make the best use of it"? For then, having dealt with this, we shall have educated ourselves to deal with a larger area.

Let me state again in other terms this fugitiveness of wealth forms, and then suggest the conclusion to which that consideration should lead us. So marked are the changes which society exhibits—especially a society in a progressive state—that the outward and visible forms which our civilisation presents to-day, its public and private buildings, its means of communication, the appliances with which it works, its machinery, its docks, its artificial harbours, its instruments of war and its instruments of peace, have most of them undergone a complete change, and many of them several complete changes, within the last sixty years. I suppose not one person in twenty in this country is living in a house which is sixty years old; not one sailor in a thousand is sailing a ship, not one artisan or labourer in a hundred is engaged in a workshop or handling tools or driving a cart which was in existence sixty years ago. It is now sixty years since the first railway was constructed from Birmingham to London, and our Railway Companies possess one thousand millions of invested capital, while our systems of water supply, of gas, of electric lighting, and of sewerage are, for the most part, of recent date. Those material relics of the past which were created more than sixty years ago, though some of them are of infinite value as mementos, examples, and heirlooms, are, for the most part, certainly not of a kind which we need wrangle over or fight about. The best of them are our universities, schools, churches, and cathedrals, and these should certainly teach us a different lesson.

But can any reasonable person, who reflects for a

moment on the recent unexampled rate of progress and invention, doubt that the next sixty years will reveal changes fully as remarkable? Can any person suppose that these mushroom forms, which have sprung up as it were in a night, have any real permanence? Even apart from the solution of the labour problem, and the finding of work for the thousands of idle hands which are eager for it—a solution, the correctness of which I claim to have demonstrated—what possibilities are opened up by the bare contemplation of the discovery of new motive powers, new means of locomotion, perhaps, through the air, new methods of water supply, or a new distribution of population, which must of itself render many material forms altogether useless and effete! Why, then, should we squabble and wrangle about what man *has* produced? Why not rather seek to learn what man *can* produce; when, aiming to do that, we may perhaps discover a grand opportunity for producing not only better forms of wealth, but how to produce them under far juster conditions? To quote the author of "Merrie England": "We should first of all ascertain what things are desirable for our health and happiness of body and mind, and then organise our people with the object of producing those things in the best and easiest way."

Wealth forms, then, in their very nature are *fugitive*, and they are besides liable to constant displacement by the better forms which in an advancing state of society are constantly arising. There is, however, one form of material wealth which is most permanent and abiding; from the value and utility of which our most wonderful inventions can never detract one jot, but will serve only to make more clear, and to render more universal. The planet on which we live has lasted for millions of years, and the race is just emerging from its savagery. Those of us who believe that there is a grand purpose behind nature cannot believe that the career of this planet is likely to be speedily cut short now that better hopes are rising in the hearts of men, and that, having learned a few of its less obscure secrets, they are finding their way, through much toil and pain, to a more noble use of its infinite treasures. The earth for all practical purposes may be regarded as abiding for ever.

Now, as every form of wealth must rest on the earth as its foundation, and must be built up out of the constituents found at or near its surface, it follows (because foundations are ever of primary importance) that the reformer should first consider how best the earth may be used in the service of man. But here again our friends, the Socialists, miss the essential point. Their professed ideal is to make society the owner of land *and of all instruments of production*; but they have been so anxious to carry both points of their programme that they have been a little too slow to consider the special importance of the land question, and have thus missed the true path of reform.

There is, however, a type of reformers who push the land question very much to the front, though, as it appears to me, in a manner little likely to commend their views to society. Mr. Henry George, in his well-known work, "Progress and Poverty," urges with much eloquence, if not with complete accuracy of reasoning, that our land laws are responsible for all the economic evils of society, and that as our landlords are little better than pirates and robbers, the sooner the State forcibly appropriates their rents the better, for when this is accomplished the problem of poverty will, he suggests, be entirely solved. But is not this attempt to throw the whole blame of and punishment for the present deplorable condition of society on to a single class of men a very great mistake? In what way are landlords as a class less honest than the average citizen? Give the average citizen the opportunity of becoming a landlord and of appropriating the land values created by his tenants, and he will embrace it to-morrow. If then, the average man is a potential landlord, to attack landlords as individuals is very like a nation drawing up an indictment against itself, and then making a scape-goat of a particular class.[1]

But to endeavour to change our land system is a very different matter from attacking those individuals who represent it. But how is this change to be effected? I reply—By the force of example, that is, by setting up a better system, and by a little skill in the grouping of forces and manipulation of ideas. It is quite true that the average man is a potential landlord, and as ready to appropriate the unearned increment as to cry out against its appropriation. But the average man has very little chance of ever becoming a landlord and of appropriating rent-values created by others; and he is, therefore, the better able to consider, quite dispassionately, whether such a proceeding is really honest, and whether it may not be possible to gradually establish a new and more equitable system under which, without enjoying the privilege of appropriating rent-values created by others,

[1] I hope it is not ungrateful in one who has derived much inspiration from "Progress and Poverty" to write thus.

he may himself be secured against expropriation of the rent-values which he is now constantly creating or maintaining. We have demonstrated how this may be done on a small scale; we have next to consider how the experiment may be carried out on a much wider scale, and this we can best do in another chapter.

CHAPTER XII.

SOCIAL CITIES.

"Human nature will not flourish, any more than a potato, if it be planted and re-planted for too long a series of generations in the same worn-out soil. My children have had other birthplaces, and, so far as their fortunes may be within my control, shall strike their roots into unaccustomed earth."—"The Scarlet Letter," Nathaniel Hawthorne.

THE problem with which we have now to deal, shortly stated, is this: How to make our Garden City experiment the stepping-stone to a higher and better form of industrial life generally throughout the country. Granted the success of the initial experiment, and there must inevitably arise a widespread demand for an extension of methods so healthy and so advantageous; and it will be well, therefore, to consider some of the chief problems which will have to be faced in the progress of such extension.

It will, I think, be well, in approaching this question, to consider the analogy presented by the early progress of railway enterprise. This will help us to see more clearly some of the broader features of the new development which is now so closely upon us if only we show ourselves energetic and imaginative. Railways were first made without any statutory powers. They were constructed on a very small scale, and, being of very short lengths, the consent of only one or at the most a few landowners was necessary; and what private agreement and arrangement could thus easily compass was scarcely a fit subject for an appeal to the Legislature of the country. But when the "Rocket" was built, and the supremacy of the locomotive was fully established, it then became necessary, if railway enterprise was to go forward, to obtain legislative powers. For it would have been impossible, or at least very difficult, to make equitable arrangements with all the landowners whose estates might lie between points many miles distant; because one obstinate landlord might take advantage of his position to demand an altogether exorbitant price for his land, and thus practically stifle such an enterprise. It was necessary, therefore, to obtain power to secure the land compulsorily at its market value, or at a price not too extravagantly removed from such value; and, this being done, railway enterprise went forward at so rapid a rate that in one year no less than £132,600,000 was authorised by Parliament to be raised for the purpose of railway construction.[1]

Now, if Parliamentary powers were necessary for the extension of railway enterprise, such powers will certainly be also needed when the inherent practicability of building new, well-planned towns, and of the population moving into them from the old slum cities as naturally, and, in proportion to the power to be exercised, almost as easily as a family moves out of a rotten old tenement into a new and comfortable dwelling, is once fairly recog-

[1] Clifford's "History of Private Bill Legislation" (Butterworth, 1885), Introduction, p. 88.

nised by the people. To build such towns, large areas of land must be obtained. Here and there a suitable site may be secured by arrangement with one or more landowners, but if the movement is to be carried on in anything like a scientific fashion, stretches of land far larger than that occupied by our first experiment must be obtained. For, just as the first short railway, which was the germ of railway enterprise, would convey to few minds the conception of a net-work of railways extending over the whole country, so, perhaps, the idea of a well-planned town such as I have described will not have prepared the reader for the later development which must inevitably follow—the planning and building of town clusters—each town in the cluster being of different design from the others, and yet the whole forming part of one large and well-thought-out plan.

Let me here introduce a very rough diagram, representing, as I conceive, the true principle on which all towns should grow. Garden City has, we will suppose, grown until it has reached a population of 32,000. How shall it grow? How shall it provide for the needs of others who will be attracted by its numerous advantages? Shall it build on the zone of agricultural land which is around it, and thus for ever destroy its right to be called a "Garden City"? Surely not. This disastrous result would indeed take place if the land around the town were, as is the land around our present cities, owned by private individuals anxious to make a profit out of it. For then, as the town filled up, the agricultural land would become "ripe" for building purposes, and the beauty and healthfulness of the town would be quickly destroyed. But the land around Garden City is, fortunately, not in the

No. 4.

ADELAIDE

SHOWING PARK LANDS ALL ROUND CITY, AND ITS MODE OF GROWTH.

No. 5.

DIAGRAM

ILLUSTRATING CORRECT PRINCIPLE OF A CITY'S GROWTH—OPEN COUNTRY EVER NEAR AT HAND, AND RAPID COMMUNICATION BETWEEN OFF-SHOOTS.

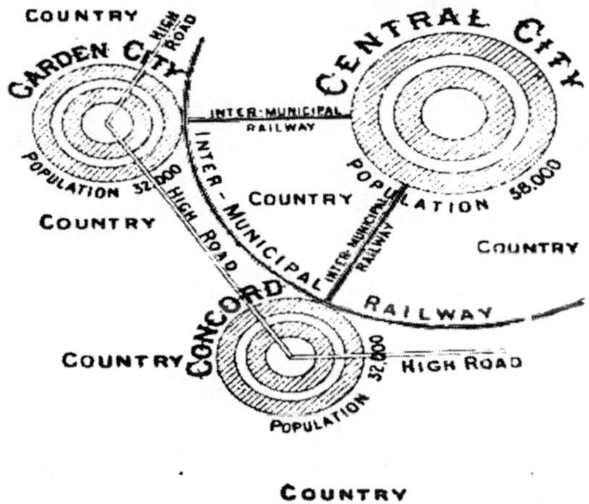

hands of private individuals: it is in the hands of the people: and is to be administered, not in the supposed interests of the few, but in the real interests of the whole community. Now, there are few objects which the people so jealously guard as their parks and open spaces; and we may, I think, feel confident that the people of Garden City will not for a moment permit the beauty of their city to be destroyed by the process of growth. But it may be urged—If this be true, will not the inhabitants of Garden City in this way be selfishly preventing the growth of their city, and thus preclude many from enjoying its advantages? Certainly not. There is a bright, but overlooked, alternative. The town *will* grow; but it will grow in accordance with a principle which will result in this—that such growth shall not lessen or destroy, but ever add to its social opportunities, to its beauty, to its convenience. Consider for a moment the case of a city in Australia which in some measure illustrates the principle for which I am contending. The city of Adelaide, as the accompanying sketch map shows, is surrounded by its "Park Lands." The city is built up. How does it grow? It grows by leaping over the "Park Lands" and establishing North Adelaide. And this is the principle which it is intended to follow, but improve upon, in Garden City.

Our diagram may now be understood. Garden City is built up. Its population has reached 32,000. How will it grow? It will grow by establishing—under Parliamentary powers probably—another city some little distance beyond its own zone of "country," so that the new town may have a zone of country of its own. I have said "by establishing another city," and, for administrative purposes there would be *two* cities; but the inhabitants of the one could reach the other in a very few minutes; for rapid transit would be specially provided for, and thus the people of the two towns would in reality represent one community.

And this principle of growth—this principle of always preserving a belt of country round our cities would be ever kept in mind till, in course of time, we should have a cluster of cities, not of course arranged in the precise geometrical form of my diagram, but so grouped around a Central City that each inhabitant of the whole group, though in one sense living in a town of small size, would be in reality living in, and would enjoy all the advantages of, a great and most beautiful city; and yet all the fresh delights of the country—field, hedgerow, and woodland—not prim parks and gardens merely—would be within a very few minutes walk or ride. And *because the people in their collective capacity own the land* on which this beautiful group of cities is built, the public buildings, the churches, the schools and universities, the libraries, picture galleries, theatres, would be on a scale of magnificence which no city in the world whose land is in pawn to private individuals can afford.

I have said that rapid railway transit would be realised by those who dwell in this beautiful city or group of cities. Reference to the diagram will show at a glance the main features of its railway system. There is, first, an inter-municipal railway connecting all the towns of the outer ring—20 miles in circumference—so that to get from any town to its most distant neighbour requires one to cover a distance of only 10 miles, which could be accomplished in, say, 12 minutes. These trains would not stop between the towns—means of communication for this purpose being afforded by electric tramways which traverse the high-roads, of which, it will be seen, there are a number—each town being connected with every other town in the group by a direct route.

There is also a system of railways by which each town is placed in direct communication with Central City. The distance from any town to the heart of Central City is only 3¼ miles, and this could be readily covered in 5 minutes.

Those who have had experience of the difficulty of getting from one suburb of London to another will see in a moment what an enormous advantage those who dwell in such a group of cities as here shown would enjoy, because they would have a railway *system* and not a railway *chaos* to serve their ends. The difficulty felt in London is of course due to want of forethought and pre-arrangement. On this point, I may quote with advantage a passage from the Presidential address of Sir Benjamin Baker to the Institute of Civil Engineers, Nov. 12th, 1895: "We Londoners often complain of the want of system in the arrangement of the railways and their terminal stations in and around the Metropolis, which necessitates our performing long journeys in cabs to get from one railway system to another. That this difficulty exists, arises, I feel sure, chiefly from the want of forethought of no less able a statesman than Sir Robert Peel, for, in 1836, a motion was proposed in the House of Commons that all the Railway Bills seeking powers for terminals in London should be referred to a Special Committee, so that a complete scheme might be evolved out of the numerous projects before Parliament, and that property might not be unnecessarily sacrificed for rival schemes. Sir Robert Peel opposed the motion on the part of the Government, on the grounds that 'no railway project could come into operation till the majority of Parliament had declared that its principles and arrangements appeared to them satisfactory, and its investments profitable. It was a recognised principle in these cases that the probable profits of an undertaking should be shown to be sufficient to maintain it in a state of permanent utility before a Bill could be obtained, and landlords were perfectly justified in expecting and demanding such a warranty from Parliament.' In this instance, incalculable injury was unintentionally inflicted upon Londoners by not having a grand central station in the Metropolis, and events have shown how false was the assumption that the passing of an Act implied any warranty as to the financial prospects of a railway."

But are the people of England to suffer for ever for the want of foresight of those who little dreamed of the future development of railways? Surely not. It was in the nature of things little likely that the first network of railways ever constructed should conform to true principles; but now, seeing the enormous progress which has been made in the means of rapid communication, it is high time that we availed ourselves more fully of those means, and built our cities upon some such plan as that I have crudely shown. We should then be, for all purposes of quick communication, nearer to each other than we are in our crowded cities, while, at the same time, we should be surrounding ourselves with the most healthy and the most advantageous conditions.

Some of my friends have suggested that such a scheme of town clusters is well enough adapted to a new country, but that in an old-settled country, with its towns built, and its railway "system" for the most part constructed, it is quite a different matter. But surely to raise such a point is to contend, in other words, that the existing wealth forms of the country are permanent, and are forever to serve as hindrances to the introduction of better forms; that crowded, ill-ventilated, unplanned, unwieldy, unhealthy cities—ulcers on the very face of our beautiful island—are to stand as barriers to the introduction of towns in which modern scientific methods and the aims of social reformers may have the fullest scope in which to express themselves. No, it cannot be; at least, it cannot be for long. What Is may hinder What Might Be for a while, but cannot stay the tide of progress. These crowded cities have done their work; they were the best which a society largely based on selfishness and rapacity could construct, but they are in the nature of things entirely unadapted for a society in which the social side of our nature is demanding a larger share of recognition—a society where even the very love of self leads us to insist upon a greater regard for the well-being of our fellows. The large cities of to-day are scarcely better adapted for the expression of the fraternal spirit than would a work on astronomy which taught that the earth was the centre of the universe be capable of adaptation for use in our schools. Each generation should build to suit its own needs; and it is no more in the nature of things that men should continue to live in old areas because their ancestors lived in them, than it is that they should cherish the old beliefs which a wider faith and a more enlarged understanding have outgrown. The reader is, therefore, earnestly asked not to take it for granted that the large cities in which he may perhaps take a pardonable pride are necessarily, in their present form, any more permanent than the stage-coach system which was the subject of so much admiration just at the very moment when it was about to be supplanted by the railways.[1] The simple issue to be faced, and faced resolutely, is—Can better results be obtained by starting on a bold plan on comparatively virgin soil than by attempting to adapt our old cities to our newer and higher needs? Thus fairly faced, the question can only be answered in one way; and when that simple fact is well grasped, the social revolution will speedily commence.

That there is ample land in this country on which such a cluster as I have here depicted could be constructed with *comparatively* small disturbance of vested interests, and, therefore, with but little need for compensation, will be obvious to anyone; and, when our first experiment has been brought to a successful issue, there will be no great difficulty in acquiring the necessary Parliamentary powers to purchase the land and carry out the necessary works step by step. County Councils are now seeking larger powers, and an overburdened Parliament is becoming more and more anxious to devolve some of its duties upon them. Let such powers be given more and more freely. Let larger and yet larger measures of local self-government be granted, and then all that my diagram depicts—only on a far better plan, because the

[1] See, for instance, the opening chapter of "The Heart of Midlothian" (Sir Walter Scott).

result of well-concerted and combined thought,—will be easily attainable.

But it may be said, "Are you not, by thus frankly avowing the very great danger to the vested interests of this country which your scheme indirectly threatens, arming vested interests against yourself, and so making any change by legislation impossible?" I think not. And for three reasons. First, because those vested interests which are said to be ranged like a solid phalanx against progress, will, by the force of circumstances and the current of events, be for once divided into opposing camps. Secondly, because property owners, who are very reluctant to yield to threats, such as are sometimes made against them by Socialists of a certain type, will be far more ready to make concessions to the logic of events as revealing itself in an undoubted advance of society to a higher form; and, thirdly, because the largest and most important, and, in the end, the most influential of all vested interests—I mean the vested interests of those who work for their living, whether by hand or brain—will be naturally in favour of the change when they understand its nature.

Let me deal with these points separately. First, I say vested-property interests will be broken in twain, and will range themselves in opposite camps. This sort of cleavage has occurred before. Thus, in the early days of railway legislation, the vested interests in canals and stage coaches were alarmed, and did all in their power to thwart and hamper what threatened them. But other great vested interests brushed this opposition easily on one side. These interests were chiefly two—capital seeking investment, and land desiring to sell itself. (A third vested interest—namely, labour seeking employment—had then scarcely begun to assert its claims.) And notice now how such a successful experiment as Garden City may easily become will drive into the very bed-rock of vested interests a great wedge, which will split them asunder with irresistible force, and permit the current of legislation to set strongly in a new direction. For what will such an experiment have proved up to the very hilt? Among other things too numerous to mention, it will have proved that far more healthy and economic conditions can be secured on raw uncultivated land (if only that land be held on just conditions) than can be secured on land which is at present of vastly higher market value; and in proving this it will open wide the doors of migration from the old crowded cities with their inflated and artificial rents, back to the land which can be now secured so cheaply. Two tendencies will then display themselves. The first will be a strong tendency for city ground values to fall, the other a less marked tendency for agricultural land to rise.[1] The holders of agricultural land, at least those who are willing to sell—and many of them are even now most anxious to do so—will welcome the extension of an experiment which promises to place English agriculture once again in a position of prosperity: the holders of city lands will, so far as their merely selfish interests prevail, greatly fear it. In this way, landowners throughout the country will be divided into two opposing factions, and the path of land reform—the foundation on which all other reforms must be built—will be made comparatively easy.

[1] The chief reason for this is that agricultural land as compared with city land is of vastly larger quantity.

Capital in the same way will be divided into opposite camps. Invested capital—that is, capital sunk in enterprises which society will recognise as belonging to the old order—will take the alarm and fall in value enormously, while, on the other hand, capital seeking investment will welcome an outlet which has long been its sorest need. Invested capital will in its opposition be further weakened by another consideration. Holders of existing forms of capital will strive—even though it be at a great sacrifice—to sell part of their old time-honoured stocks, and invest them in new enterprises, on municipally-owned land, for they will not wish to "have all their eggs in one basket"; and thus will the opposing influences of vested property neutralise each other.

But vested-property interests will be, as I believe, affected yet more remarkably in another way. The man of wealth, when he is personally attacked and denounced as an enemy of society, is slow to believe in the perfect good faith of those who denounce him, and, when efforts are made to tax him out by the forcible hand of the State, he is apt to use every endeavour, lawful or unlawful, to oppose such efforts—and often with no small measure of success. But the average wealthy man is no more an unmixed compound of selfishness than the average poor man; and if he sees his houses or lands depreciated in value, not by force, but because those who lived in or upon them have learned how to erect far better homes of their own, and on land held on conditions more advantageous to them, and to surround their children with many advantages which cannot be enjoyed on his estate, he will philosophically bow to the inevitable, and, in his better moments, even welcome a change which will involve him in far greater pecuniary loss than any change in the incidence of taxation is likely to inflict. In every man there is some measure of the reforming instinct; in every man there is some regard for his fellows; and when these natural feelings run athwart his pecuniary interests, then the result is that the spirit of opposition is inevitably softened, in some degree in all men, while in others it is entirely replaced by a fervent desire for the country's good, even at the sacrifice of many cherished possessions. Thus it is that what will not be yielded to a force from without may readily be granted as the result of an impulse from within.

And now let me deal for a moment with the greatest, the most valuable, and the most permanent of all vested interests—the vested interests of skill, labour, energy, talent, industry. How will these be affected? My answer is, The force which will divide in twain the vested interests of land and capital will unite and consolidate the interests of those who live by work, and will lead them to unite their forces with the holders of agricultural land and of capital seeking investment, to urge upon the State the necessity for the prompt opening up of facilities for the reconstruction of society; and, when the State is slow to act, then to employ voluntary collective efforts similar to those adopted in the Garden City experiment, with such modifications as experience may show to be necessary. Such a task as the construction of a cluster of cities like that represented in our diagram may well inspire all workers with that enthusiasm which unites men, for it will call for the very highest talents of engineers of all kinds, of architects, artists, medical men, experts in sanitation, landscape gardeners, agricultural experts, surveyors, builders, manufacturers, merchants and financiers, organisers of trades unions, friendly and co-operative societies, as well as the very simplest forms of unskilled labour, together with all those forms of lesser skill and talent which lie between. For the vastness of the task which seems to frighten some of my friends, represents, in fact, the very measure of its value to the community, if that task be only undertaken in a worthy spirit and with worthy aims. Work in abundance is, as has been several times urged, one of the greatest needs of to-day, and no such field of employment has been opened up since civilisation began as would be represented by the task which is before us of reconstructing anew the entire external fabric of society, employing, as we build, all the skill and knowledge which the experience of centuries has taught us. It was "a large order" which was presented in the early part of this century to construct iron highways throughout the length and breadth of this island, uniting in a vast network all its towns and cities. But railway enterprise, vast as has been its influence, touched the life of the people at but few points compared with the newer call to build home-towns for slum cities; to plant gardens for crowded courts; to construct beautiful water-ways in flooded valleys; to establish a scientific system of distribution to take the place of a chaos, a just system of land tenure for one representing the selfishness which we hope is passing away; to found pensions with liberty for our aged poor, now imprisoned in workhouses; to banish despair and awaken hope in the breasts of those who have fallen; to silence the harsh voice of anger, and to awaken the soft notes of brotherliness and goodwill; to place in strong hands implements of peace and construction, so that implements of war and destruction may drop uselessly down. Here is a task which may well unite a vast army of workers to utilise that power, the present waste of which is the source of half our poverty, disease, and suffering.

CHAPTER XIII.

THE FUTURE OF LONDON.

It will now be interesting to consider some of the more striking effects which will be produced on our now overcrowded cities by the opening-up in new districts of such a vast field of employment as the reader's mind will, it is hoped, be now able to realise with some degree of clearness. New towns and groups of towns are springing up in parts of our islands hitherto well-nigh deserted; new means of communication, the most scientific the world has yet seen, are being constructed; new means of distribution are bringing the producer and the consumer into closer relations, and thus (by reducing railway rates and charges, and the number of profits) are at once raising prices to the producer and diminishing them to the consumer; parks and gardens, orchards and woods, are being planted in the midst of the busy life of the people, so that they may be enjoyed in the fullest measure; homes are being erected for those who have long lived in slums; work is found for the workless, land for the landless, and opportunities for the expenditure of long pent-up energy are presenting themselves at every turn. A new sense of freedom and joy is pervading the hearts of the people as their individual faculties are awakened, and they discover, in a social life which permits alike of the completest concerted action and of the fullest individual liberty, the long-sought-for means of reconciliation between order and freedom—between the well-being of the individual and of society.

The effects produced on our over-crowded cities, whose forms are at once, by the light of a new contrast, seen to be old-fashioned and effete, will be so far-reaching in their character that, in order to study them effectively, it will be well to confine our attention to London, which, as the largest and most unwieldy of our cities, is likely to exhibit those effects in the most marked degree.

There is, as I said at the outset, a well-nigh universal current of opinion that a remedy for the depopulation of our country districts and for the overcrowding of our large cities is urgently needed. But though every one recommends that a remedy should be diligently sought for, few appear to believe that such a remedy will ever be found, and the calculations of our statesmen and reformers proceed upon the assumption that not only will the tide of population never actually turn from the large cities countryward, but that it will continue to flow in its present direction at a scarcely diminished rate for a long time to come.[1] Now it can hardly be supposed that any

[1] It is scarcely necessary to give instances of what is meant; but one that occurs to my mind is that this assumption of the continued growth of London forms one of the fundamental premises of the Report of the Royal Commission on Metropolitan Water Supply, 1893. On the contrary, it is satisfactory to note that Mr. H. G. Wells has recently entirely changed his views as to the future growth of London (*see* "Anticipations," chap. ii.). Read also "The Distribution of Industry," by P. W. Wilson, in "the Heart of the Empire" (Fisher Unwin), and Paper by Mr. W. L. Madgen, M.I.E.E., on "Industrial Redistribution," *Society of Arts Journal*, February, 1902. *See* also note on page 31.

search made in the full belief that the remedy sought for will not be discovered is likely to be carried on with great zeal or thoroughness; and, therefore, it is perhaps not surprising to find that though the late chairman of the London County Council (Lord Rosebery) declared that the growth of this huge city was fitly comparable to the growth of a tumour (*see* p. 11)—few venturing to deny the correctness of the analogy—yet the various members of that body, instead of bending their energies to reforming London by means of a reduction of its population, are boldly advocating a policy which involves the purchase of vast undertakings on behalf of the municipality, at prices which must prove far higher than they will be worth if only the long-sought-for remedy is found.

Let us now assume (simply as an hypothesis, if the reader is still sceptical) that the remedy advocated in this work is effective; that new garden-cities are springing up all over the country on sites owned by the municipalities—the rate-rents of such corporate property forming a fund ample for the carrying on of municipal undertakings representing the highest skill of the modern engineer and the best aspirations of the enlightened reformer; and that in these cities, healthier, wholesomer, cleaner and more just and sound economic conditions prevail. What, then, must in the nature of things be the more noticeable effects upon London and the population of London; upon its land values; upon its municipal debt, and its municipal assets; upon London as a labour market; upon the homes of its people; upon its open spaces, and upon the great undertakings which our socialistic and municipal reformers are at the present moment so anxious to secure?

First, notice that ground values will fall enormously! Of course, so long as the 121 square miles out of the 58,000 square miles of England exercise a magnetic attraction so great as to draw to it one-fifth of the whole population, who compete fiercely with each other for the right to occupy the land within that small area, so long will that land have a monopoly price. But de-magnetise that people, convince large numbers of them that they can better their condition in every way by migrating elsewhere, and what becomes of that monopoly value? Its spell is broken, and the great bubble bursts.

But the life and earnings of Londoners are not only in pawn to the owners of its soil, who kindly permit them to live upon it at enormous rents—£16,000,000 per annum, representing the present ground value of London, which is yearly increasing; but they are also in pawn to the extent of about £40,000,000, representing London's municipal debts.

But notice this. A municipal debtor is quite different from an ordinary debtor in one most important respect. *He can escape payment by migration.* He has but to move away from a given municipal area, and he at once, *ipso facto,* shakes off not only all his obligations to his landlord, but also all his obligations to his municipal creditors. It is true, when he migrates he must assume the burden of a new municipal rent, and of a new municipal debt; but these in our new cities will represent an extremely small and diminishing fraction of the burden now borne, and the temptation to migrate will, for this and many other reasons, be extremely strong.

But now let us notice how each person in migrating

from London, while making the burden of *ground-rents* less heavy for those who remain, will (unless there be some change in the law), make the burden of *rates* on the ratepayers of London yet heavier. For, though each person in migrating will enable those who remain to make better and yet better terms with their landlords; on the other hand, the municipal debt remaining the same, the interest on it will have to be borne by fewer and yet fewer people, and thus the relief to the working population which comes from *reduced rent* will be largely discounted by *increased rates*, and in this way the temptation to migrate will continue, and yet further population will remove, making the debt ever a larger and larger burden, till at length, though accompanied by a still further reduction of rent, it may become intolerable. Of course this huge debt need never have been incurred. Had London been built on municipally-owned land, its rents would not only have easily provided for all current expenditure, without any need for a levy of rates or for incurring loans for long periods, but it would have been enabled to own its own water-supply and many other useful and profit-bearing undertakings, instead of being in its present position with vast debts and small assets. But a vicious and immoral system is bound ultimately to snap, and when the breaking-point is reached, the owners of London's bonds will, like the owners of London's land, have to make terms with a people who can apply the simple remedy of migrating and building a better and brighter civilisation elsewhere, if they are not allowed to rebuild on a just and reasonable basis on the site of their ancient city.

We may next notice, very briefly, the bearing of this

migration of population upon two great problems—the problem of the housing of the people of London, and the problem of finding employment for those who remain. The rents now paid by the working population of London, for accommodation most miserable and insufficient, represents each year a larger and larger proportion of income, while the cost of moving to and from work, continually increasing, often represents in time and money a very considerable tax. But imagine the population of London falling, and falling rapidly; the migrating people establishing themselves where rents are extremely low, and where their work is within easy-walking distance of their homes! Obviously, house-property in London will fall in rental value, and fall enormously. Slum property will sink to zero, and the whole working population will move into houses of a class quite above those which they can now afford to occupy. Families which are now compelled to huddle together in one room will be able to rent five or six, and thus will the housing problem temporarily solve itself by the simple process of a diminution in the numbers of the tenants.

But what will become of this slum property? Its power to extort a large proportion of the hard earnings of the London poor gone for ever, will it yet remain an eye-sore and a blot, though no longer a danger to health and an outrage on decency? No. These wretched slums will be pulled down, and their sites occupied by parks, recreation grounds, and allotment gardens. And this change, as well as many others, will be effected, not at the expense of the ratepayers, but almost entirely at the expense of the landlord class: in this sense, at least, that such ground rents as are still paid by the people of London in respect of those classes of property which retain some rental value will have to bear the burden of improving the city. Nor will, I think, the compulsion of any Act of Parliament be necessary to effect this result: it will probably be achieved by the voluntary action of the landowners, compelled, by a Nemesis from whom there is no escape, to make some restitution for the great injustice which they have so long committed.

For observe what must inevitably happen. A vast field of employment being opened outside London, unless a corresponding field of employment is opened within it, London must die,—when the landowners will be in a sorry plight. Elsewhere new cities are being built: London then must be transformed. Elsewhere the town is invading the country: here the country must invade the town. Elsewhere cities are being built on the terms of paying low prices for land, and of then vesting such land in the new municipalities: in London corresponding arrangements must be made or no one will consent to build. Elsewhere, owing to the fact that there are but few interests to buy out, improvements of all kinds can go forward rapidly and scientifically: in London similar improvements can only be carried out if vested interests recognise the inevitable and accept terms which may seem ridiculous, but are no more so than those which a manufacturer often finds himself compelled to submit to, who sells for a ridiculously low price the machine which has cost a very large sum, for the simple reason that there is a far better one in the market, and that it no longer *pays*, in the face of keen competition, to work the inferior machine. The displacement of capital will, no doubt, be enormous, but the implacement of labour will be yet greater. A few may be made comparatively poor, but the many will be made comparatively rich a very healthy change, the slight evils attending which society will be well able to mitigate.

There are already visible symptoms of the coming change—rumblings which precede the earthquake. London at this very moment may be said to be on strike against its landowners. Long-desired London improvements are awaiting such a change in the law as will throw some of the cost of making them upon the landowners of London. Railways are projected, but in some cases are not built—for instance, The Epping Forest Railway—because the London County Council, most properly anxious to keep down the fares by workmen's trains, press for and secure, at the hands of a Parliamentary Committee, the imposition of terms upon the promoters which seem to them extremely onerous and unremunerative, but which would pay the company extremely well were it not for the prohibitive price asked for land and other property along the line of its projected route. These checks upon enterprise must affect the growth of London even now, and make it less rapid than it otherwise would be; but when the untold treasures of our land are unlocked, and when the people now living in London discover how easily vested interests, without being attacked, may be circumvented, then the landowners of London and those who represent other vested interests had better quickly make terms, or London, besides being what Mr. Grant Allen termed "a squalid village," will also become a deserted one.

But better counsels, let us hope, will prevail, and a

new city rise on the ashes of the old. The task will indeed be difficult. Easy, comparatively, is it to lay out on virgin soil the plan of a magnificent city, such as represented on our Diagram 5. Of far greater difficulty is the problem—even if all vested interests freely effaced themselves—of rebuilding a new city on an old site, and that site occupied by a huge population. But this, at least, is certain, that the present area of the London County Council ought not (if health and beauty, and that which is too frequently put in the front rank—rapid production of wealth forms—are to be considered) to contain more than, say, one-fifth of its present population; and that new systems of railways, sewerage, drainage, lighting, parks, etc., must be constructed if London is to be saved, while the whole system of production and of distribution must undergo changes as complete and as remarkable as was the change from a system of barter to our present complicated commercial system.

Proposals for the reconstruction of London have already been projected. In 1883 the late Mr. William Westgarth offered the Society of Arts the sum of £1,200 to be awarded in prizes for essays on the best means of providing dwellings for the London poor, and on the reconstruction of Central London—an offer which brought forward several schemes of some boldness.[1] More recently a book by Mr. Arthur Cawston, entitled "A Comprehensive Scheme for Street Improvements in London," was published by Stanford, which contains in its introduction the following striking passage:—"The literature relating to London, extensive as it is, contains

[1] *See* "Reconstruction of Central London" (George Bell and Sons).

no work which aims at the solution of one problem of vast interest to Londoners. They are beginning to realise, partly by their more and more extensive travels, and partly through their American and foreign critics, that the gigantic growth of their capital, without the controlling guidance of a municipality, has resulted in not only the biggest, but in probably the most irregular, inconvenient, and unmethodical collection of houses in the world. A comprehensive plan for the transformation of Paris has been gradually developed since 1848; slums have disappeared from Berlin since 1870; eighty-eight acres in the centre of Glasgow have been remodelled; Birmingham has transformed ninety-three acres of squalid slums into magnificent streets flanked by architectural buildings; Vienna, having completed her stately outer ring, is about to remodel her inner city: and the aim of the writer is to show, by example and illustration, in what way the means successfully employed for improving these cities can be best adapted to the needs of London."

The time for the complete reconstruction of London—which will eventually take place on a far more comprehensive scale than that now exhibited in Paris, Berlin, Glasgow, Birmingham, or Vienna—has, however, not yet come. A simpler problem must first be solved. One small Garden City must be built as a working model, and then a group of cities such as that dealt with in the last chapter. These tasks done, and done well, the reconstruction of London must inevitably follow, and the power of vested interests to block the way will have been almost, if not entirely, removed.

Let us, therefore, first bend all our energies to the smaller of these tasks, thinking only of the larger tasks which lie beyond as incentives to a determined line of immediate action, and as a means of realising the great value of little things if done in the right manner and in the right spirit.

THE END.

INDEX

I

J

K

L

M

N

O

P

R

S

T

U

V

W

POSTSCRIPT.

"To-Morrow," of which this book is substantially a reproduction, having been published towards the end of 1898, the reader who has followed me thus far will be interested to learn what has been done, and what is proposed to be done to realise the project which was there set forth. I will endeavour to answer these questions.

At the outset, I perceived that the first thing was to make the project widely known—that the city which was pictured so vividly in my own mind must be pictured more or less vividly by many, and that a strong and widespread desire for its up-rearing must be created before a single step could be wisely taken to put the project in a concrete form. For the task before me was, I was fully conscious, a most difficult one, and demanded the hearty co-operation of men and of women[1] experienced in very numerous departments of human activity; and many of these had to be reached and enlisted. City building, as a deliberately thought-out enterprise, is indeed a lost art, in this country at least, and this art has not only to be revived, but has to be carried to finer issues than those who have before practised it ever dreamt of. Autocrats like Alexander the Great and Philip II. could build cities according to

[1] Woman's influence is too often ignored. When Garden City is built, as it shortly will be, woman's share in the work will be found to have been a large one. Women are among our most active missionaries.

well-thought out and carefully-matured plans, because they could impose their will by force; but a city which is to be the outward expression of a strong desire to secure the best interests of all its inhabitants can, among a self-governing people, only arise as the outcome of much patient and well-sustained effort. Moreover, the building of the first of such cities necessarily involves co-operation on new lines—in untried ways; and, as it is essential that the freedom of the individual as well as the interests of the community should be preserved, very much work must needs be done to prepare the way for the successful launching of such an experiment.

My task—hardly a self-imposed one, for, when I commenced my investigations many years ago, I little dreamed where they would lead me—was rendered especially difficult by the nature of my professional work, which it was impossible for me to give up; and I could, therefore, only give odds and ends of time and energies largely exhausted to the work. But, fortunately, I was not left without help. First the press came to my aid. "To-Morrow" was very widely noticed. Many books have been more fully reviewed, but few have been noticed, and favourably noticed, in such a variety of types of journals as "To-Morrow" has been. Besides the daily and weekly papers of London and the provinces, the project has been favourably commented upon in journals representing widely different points of view. I may mention, merely as illustrations of this—"Commerce," "Country Gentleman," "Spectator," "Leisure Hour," "Court Circular," "Clarion," "Builder's Journal," "Commonwealth," "Young Man," "Councillor and Guardian," "Ladies' Pictorial,"

"Public Health Engineer," "Municipal Journal," "Argus," "Vegetarian," "Journal of Gas Lighting," "Labour Copartnership," "Hospital," "Brotherhood," "Municipal Reformer."

Nor was the reason of this widespread interest difficult to discover. The project, indeed, touches life at every point, and when once carried out will be an object-lesson which must have far-reaching and beneficial results.

But, although approval of my aims was general, doubts were often, especially at first, expressed as to their realisability. Thus, the "Times" said: "The details of administration, taxation, etc., work out to perfection. The only difficulty is to create the city, but that is a small matter to Utopians." If this be so, then, by the "Times'" own showing, I am no Utopian, for to me the building of the city is what I have long set my mind upon, and it is with me no "small matter." A few months after this, however, the "Journal of Gas Lighting" put my case very forcibly thus: "Why should the creation of a town be an insuperable difficulty. It is nothing of the kind. Materials for a tentative realisation of Mr Howard's ideal city exist in abundance in London at the present moment. Time and again it is anounced that some London firm have transferred their factory to Rugby, or Dunstable, or High Wycombe for business reasons. It ought not to be impossible to systematise this movement and give the old country some new towns in which intelligent design shall direct the social workings of economic forces."

In my spare time I lectured on the Garden City, the first lecture after publication being given in December, 1898, at the Rectory Road Congregational Church, Stoke Newington, N. In the chair was Mr. T. E. Young, past President, Institute of Actuaries, and I was supported also by Dr. Forman, A.L.C.C.; Rev. C. Fleming Williams, A.L.C.C.; Mr. James Branch, L.C.C.; and Mr. Lampard, L.C.C. The lecture was well reported in a local journal, and I speedily found that, by means of lectures, interest in the project could be widened, because the subject made "good copy." I, therefore, as far as possible, have always given lectures when requested, and have spoken in London, Glasgow, Manchester, and many provincial towns. Friends, too, began to help, the Rev. J. Bruce Wallace, M.A., of Brotherhood Church being among the first to lecture upon the project; nor shall I ever forget the pleasure I felt at hearing his simple and forcible exposition of it.

Soon after the publication of "To-Morrow," I began to receive many letters, and these often from business men. One of the first of these was from Mr. W. R. Bootland, of Daisy Bank Mills, Newchurch, near Warrington, who wrote heartily commending the project as "sound business," and yet as likely to confer great public benefits.

After a few months of such fitful work as I could undertake, I consulted a friend, Mr F. W. Flear, and we decided it would be well to form an Association with a view to securing supporters in a more systematic manner, and of formulating the scheme more completely, so that, at as early a date as possible, a suitable organisation might be created for carrying it out. Accordingly, on the 10th June, 1899, a few friends met at the offices of Mr. Alexander W. Payne, Chartered Accountant, 70

Finsbury Pavement, E.C., Mr Fred. Bishop, of Tunbridge Wells, in the chair, and the Garden City Association was formed—Mr. Payne being its first Hon. Treasurer, and Mr. F. W. Steere, a barrister, who had written a very useful summary of "To-Morrow" in *Uses*, its first Hon. Secretary. On the 21st of the same month, a public meeting was held at the Memorial Hall, Farringdon Street, E.C., which was presided over by Sir John Leng, M.P., who, at a very short notice, gave an interesting outline of the project, and urged those present to support me in my very difficult task. At this meeting a Council was formed, and at the first sittings of that body Mr. T. H. W. Idris, J.P., L.C.C., was elected chairman, a post which he resigned at a later stage on account of ill-health, though remaining as firmly convinced as ever of the soundness of the Garden City idea.

Lecturers now began to come forward in different parts of the country, and additional interest was afforded by lantern slides and diagrams. The Association steadily grew, and three months after its formation I was able to write to the "Citizen":—"The Association numbers amongst its members, Manufacturers, Co-operators, Architects, Artists, Medical Men, Financial Experts, Lawyers, Merchants, Ministers of Religion, Members of the L.C.C., Moderate and Progressive; Socialists and Individuals, Radicals and Conservatives."

Our subscriptions, however, were very small. We had put the minimum at the democratic shilling, so that none should be shut out, but, unfortunately, some who could afford much more were content to subscribe that sum, and, from the formation of the Association until August 13, 1901—a little more than two years—the total subscriptions to the general funds of the Association only reached £241 13s. 9d.

A change suddenly came over the Association. I learned early in 1901 that Mr. Ralph Neville, K.C., had written in "Labour Copartnership" expressing his full approval of the essential principles of the Garden City project, and when I called upon him he at once consented to join our Council, and, shortly afterwards, was unanimously elected its chairman. At about the same time, though our financial position hardly justified such a step, we took an office of our own, and engaged a paid secretary, who agreed to devote his whole time to the work.

And here the Garden City Association was very fortunate. It secured the services of Mr. Thomas Adams, a young Scotchman, who has proved active, energetic, and resourceful—to whose suggestion was due the Conference held last September at Mr. Cadbury's beautiful village of Bournville, which has done more than anything else to make the Garden City Association and its project known to the great public, and to give to our members ocular proof of the feasibility—indeed, the wonderful success—of a scheme in so many respects like our own.*

Since our Annual Meeting in December our membership has increased—thanks mainly to a special effort of members—from 530 to 1,300; and, as many of our friends, anxious to put the project to the test of experiment at an early date, are offering to subscribe very considerable sums, a Joint Stock Company, to be called the

* Through the kindness of Messrs. Lever Brothers, a conference is being arranged for July this year at Port Sunlight, a most admirably planned industrial village in Cheshire.

Garden City Pioneer Company, Limited, with a small capital of about £20,000, is being formed for the purpose of securing the option of a site, and of preparing and presenting to the public a complete scheme adapted to the development of the site thus selected—a scheme which will be in accordance with the general principles set forth in this book, but differing, of course, in many details. Subscribers to this preliminary Company will, of course, run considerable risk; and, as the profits, even in the event of the most complete success, will only be nominal, the appeal will be addressed only to those who take an interest in the project as public-spirited citizens. The Secretary of the Garden City Association will give the latest information on this subject, and will also gladly enrol members.

No one can possibly be under a greater obligation than he who has an idea which he earnestly wishes to see carried out and who finds others helping him to make visible that which exists only as a thought. Under this greatest of debts am I. By writing; by speaking; by organising public meetings and drawing-room meetings; by suggestion, encouragement, and advice; by secretarial and other work; by making the project known among their friends; by subscribing funds for propaganda work; and, now, by offering to subscribe considerable sums for practical steps, many have helped and are helping me to do that which, without their aid, must have been quite impossible. They have thus multiplied my strength a thousandfold; and from the very bottom of my heart I thank them for the assurance of speedy success which their efforts have thus given me. Ere long, I trust we shall meet in Garden City.

GARDEN CITY ASSOCIATION.

VICE-PRESIDENTS.

The Countess of Warwick.
The Earl of Carrington, G.C.M.G., L.C.C.
The Earl of Meath, L.C.C.
The Bishop of London.
The Bishop of Hereford.
The Bishop of Rochester.
Percy Alden, M.A.
Dr. Tempest Anderson (York).
Yarborough Anderson.
L. A. Atherley-Jones, K.C., M.P.
William Baker.
R. A. Barrett (Ashton-under-Lyne).
J. Williams Benn, J.P., L.C.C.
Sir M. M. Bhownaggree, K.C.I.E., M.P.
W. R. Bootland (Manchester).
Rev. Stopford Brooke, M.A.
The Right Hon. James Bryce, M.P.
W. P. Byles, J.P. (Bradford).
George Cadbury, J.P. (Bournville).
W. S. Caine, M.P.
Robert Cameron, M.P.
Professor Chapman (Manchester).
Rev. Thomas Child.
Dr. John Clifford, M.A.
Miss Marie Corelli.
Walter Crane.
Alderman W. H. Dickinson, L.C.C.
Canon Moore Ede (Sunderland).
Samuel Edwards, J.P. (Birmingham).
The Master of Elibank, M.P.
Alfred Emmott, M.P.
F. J. Farquharson, J.P.
Mrs. Anna Farquharson.
Michael Flürscheim.
Lady Forsyth.
Sir Walter Foster, M.P.
Madame Sarah Grand.
Corrie Grant, M.P.
W. Winslow Hall, M.D., M.R.C.S.
G. A. Hardy, L.C.C.
Cecil Harmsworth.
R. Leicester Harmsworth, M.P.
Henry B. Harris.
Anthony Hope Hawkins.
The Hon. Claude G. Hay, M.P.
Sir Robert Head, Bart.
C. E. Hobhouse, M.P.
Henry Holiday.
Canon Scott Holland.
George Jacob Holyoake.
Rev. Alfred Hood.
T. H. W. Idris, J.P.
Ben. Jones (Chairman C.W.S. London).
Mrs. Ashton Jonson.
Dean Kitchin (Durham).
George Lampard, L.C.C.
A. L. Leon, L.C.C.
Sir John Leng, M.P.
W. H. Lever (Port Sunlight).
J. W. Logan, M.P.
Dr. T. J. Macnamara, M.P.
Walter T. Macnamara.
Mrs. Magrath.
R. Biddulph Martin, M.P.
Professor Alfred Marshall (Cambridge).
Rev. F. B. Meyer
Edward R. P. Moon, M.P.
Mrs. Morgan-Browne.
Harington Morgan.
The Hon Dadabhai Naoroji.
Mrs. Overy.
Gilbert Parker, M.P.
F. Platt-Higgins, M.P.
Sir Robert Pullar (Perth).
Joseph Rowntree (York).
C. E. Schwann, M.P.
Arthur Sherwell.
Albert Spicer, J.P.
Henry C. Stephens, J.P.
Miss Julie Sutter.
A. C. Swinton.
Ivor H. Tuckett (Cambridge).
J. Elliott Viney.
Professor A. R. Wallace, D.C.L., F.R.S.
J. Bruce Wallace, M.A.
H. G. Wells.
Richard Whiteing.
J. H. Whitley, M.P.
Aneurin Williams.
Alderman Rev. Fleming Williams, L.C.C.
Robert Williams, F.R.I.B.A., L.C.C.
Henry J. Wilson, M.P.
Wm. Woodward, A.R.I.B.A.
Robert Yerburgh, M.P.
T. E. Young, B.A., F.R.A.S.
J. H. Yoxall, M.P.

GARDEN CITY ASSOCIATION.

COUNCIL.

Chairman—Ralph Neville, K.C. *Hon. Treasurer*—A. W. Payne, F.C.A., F.S.S.

A. S. E. Ackerman, A.M. Inst. C.E.
C. M. Bailhache, LL.B.
G. M. Bishop.
Arthur Blott.
Miss Edith Bradley (Lady Warwick Hostel).
James Branch, J.P., L.C.C.
William Carter.
J. Cleghorn.
G. Crosoer.
F. W. Flear.
J. C. Gray (Secretary, Co-op. Union Manchester).
Ebenezer Howard.
Mrs. Ebenezer Howard.
James P. Hurst.
H. C. Lander, A.R.I.B.A.
Fred. W. Lawrence, M.A.
H. D. Pearsall, M.Inst.C.E.
T. P. Ritzema, J.P. (Blackburn).
Edward Rose.
Hon. Rollo Russell.
W. H. Gurney Salter.
Sydney Schiff (Chester).
W. S. Sherrington, M.A., L.L.M.
Edward T. Sturdy.
Alderman W. Thompson.
Herbert Warren, B.A.
Aneurin Williams.

(The full Council will consist of 30 Members.)

Honorary Provincial Secretaries.

Manchester District—R. Morrell, Moston Lane, New Moston, Manchester.
Liverpool and Cheshire District—J. Norton, 1 Morningside Road, Bootle, near Liverpool.
N.E.—F. W. Bricknell, Guyscliffe, Hessle, East Yorks.
Midlands—Rev. J. B. Higham, 25 Copthorne Road, Wolverhampton.
Scotland—{ Robert MacLaurin, 39 Caldercuilt Road, Maryhill, Glasgow. James Allport, 15 Montpelier, Edinburgh.

General Secretary—

THOMAS ADAMS, 77 Chancery Lane, London, W.C.

Objects.

To promote the discussion of the project suggested by Mr. Ebenezer Howard in "To-morrow"*, and ultimately to formulate a practical scheme on the lines of that project, with such modifications as may appear desirable.

Membership.

Payment of an Annual Subscription of not less than 1s. confers Membership. A Subscription of 2s. 6d., or more, entitles the Subscriber to all literature published by the Association. More funds are required for the immediate purpose of bringing our proposals prominently before the public, and an average subscription of 5s. per member is necessary to meet current expenditure. The income for

* Now published by Swan Sonnenschein & Co. (London), under the title "Garden Cities of To-morrow."

the first half year 1901-02 was ten times that of the same period of the previous year. The Membership is over 1,300, being an increase of 700 since January 1st, 1902. It is hoped that all who are desirous of improving, by constitutional means, the present physical, social, and industrial conditions of life in town and country, will help to immediately increase this number.

Sectional Committees.

Committees have been or are being appointed to consider questions of detail, such as Land Tenure, Manufactures and Trade, Co-operative Societies, Labour, Housing and Public Health, Liquor Traffic, Education, Smoke Abatement, Art, etc. Members desirous of taking part in the work of any section are requested to communicate with the General Secretary.

Publications.

The Association publishes a number of tracts which are forwarded to members on joining. A list of publications and some explanatory literature will be sent free on application. A few reports of the Bournville Conference may still be had, price 6d., post free. These reports consist of 80 pages, and contain reports of speeches by—Earl Grey, Mr. Ralph Neville, K.C.; Mr. George Cadbury, Mr. Aneurin Wililams, the Mayor of Camberwell, Sir M. M. Bhownaggree, M.P.; Mr. R. B. Martin, M.P.; Mr. Ebenezer Howard, Dr. Mansfield Robinson, and others.

All communications should be addressed to the Secretary, Garden City Association, 77 Chancery Lane, London, W.C. Cheques and postal orders should be crossed London City and Midland Bank, Fore Street.